Renaissance Leadership

Rethinking and Leading the Future

Stephen Murgatroyd, PhD and D.G. Simpson, PhD

Murgatroyd, Stephen 1950-
Simpson, Donald G 1934-

Renaissance Leadership – Rethinking and Leading the Future

ISBN: 978-0-557-95867-2

If the ideas outlined here of interest, then you can read more at www.innovationexpedition.com

First printing in March 2010

From Stephen Murgatroyd, PhD FBPsS FRSA

Dedicated to Donald G. Simpson, PhD

Friend, Colleague, Mentor, Imagineer, Pioneer

From Donald G. Simpson, PhD

Dedicated to Peter F. Drucker

A Modern Day Renaissance Leader who Inspired Us

Innovation Expedition Inc.
Rethinking and Leading the Future

CONTENTS

Preface

"The ideal manager must have a truly Renaissance view of his role if he expects to succeed. The term "Renaissance Man" was coined in the late Middle Ages to describe the person who is skilled and well versed in all of the arts and sciences. It assumes an open mind, a willingness to learn constantly, an attitude of constant self-renewal, an awareness of other values and cultures and a keen political awareness."

—W. J. Light and J. W. Brown Competing Successfully in the International Marketplace

This book is a brief introduction to the ideas driving the concept of renaissance leadership for the global knowledge economy as co-created by the *Innovation Expedition* and a number of its alliance partners over the last two decades.

The Leadership Challenge of the Knowledge Economy

It is becoming increasingly clear that the type of leadership that drove organizational success in the Industrial Era will not be sufficient for the Knowledge Era, especially after the 2008-9 recession and the global "shakeout" that has followed.

What kind of leadership, then, will offer the greatest chance in this fast changing world of harnessing the creative energy required to drive dramatic improvements in organizational performance, deliver harmonious prosperity and support the development of a satisfying quality of life for our community and others around the globe?

Over the past several years the *Innovation Expedition* has been on a journey to discover what knowing, doing and being skills are required to lead successful, high performing, knowledge-based organizations. We believe it is a style of entrepreneurial, collaborative and innovative leadership we call Renaissance

Leadership. We believe that the shift to a knowledge economy is a significant period of "rebirth" akin to the great Renaissance periods of the past, and shares with them an intense focus on learning and inquiry encompassing all aspects of human life. We believe that the world is in the midst of a new renaissance.

What do we mean by the term, Renaissance Leader?

The *Innovation Expedition* describes Renaissance Leaders as high integrity individuals with sensitive self-awareness and a passion both for driving high performance in their organizations and for helping to make their communities and the world a better place.

These leaders have a sense of history and an unusual capacity for viewing the world holistically, for practicing systems thinking, for injecting a global and a future's perspective into present challenges, for honouring diversity, and for drawing on ideas and best practices from diverse disciplines and economic sectors.

They also demonstrate an ability to take the input from these various disciplines, synthesize it and integrate it for application to a specific complex task.

Finally, they have mastered the art of demonstrating grace under pressure, and of inspiring others to have the courage to collaborate and innovate in order to dramatically improve organizational performance.

Utilizing the Renaissance Concept as a Metaphor and a Model

We are using the term "Renaissance" as a powerful rallying call for creative change in periods of major paradigm shifts. We want to identify and support those leaders who are moved to action by awareness of the lessons from earlier Renaissance periods and by a desire to emulate the behaviour of some of these leadership heroes from an earlier age.

The world has seen many "renaissances"—literally periods of rebirth, rejuvenation or reawakening in which a spirit of courageous, creative, open inquiry inspires breakthroughs in the arts, sciences, technology and business. This type of leadership in periods of major change ultimately leads to fundamental changes to economic, political and social models. The thinking outlined in this book draws on lessons from an iconic historical Renaissance in Europe and uses them to inspire modern day Renaissance leadership.

The book is based on the following core assumptions:

1. **The world is changing in three distinct ways:**

   a. The nature of economic power is shifting from the major dominance of the US/Europe to include some emerging economies such as Brazil, Russia, India, China and this will lead to *changes in the nature of socio-economic transactions in the world.*

   b. The environment of the world (climate, access to water, biodiversity) is changing, becoming a real issue which organizations have to address. Climate change is one aspect of this, but the key issue is *environmental responsibility.*

   c. The relationship of the individual to their community and society is changing in a paradoxical way. At the same time as *the person is increasingly disconnected from society because of the increasing complexity of institutions and systems they are experiencing, they have more connections through self-constructed "communities" or social networks which matter to them.*

2. **Organizations, especially for profit organizations, are seeing their operational landscape change**—Global supply chains and free trade are creating more complex markets and systems requiring leaders to develop *an increased understanding of global factors which impact*

their operations. The recent recession demonstrated that market failures in one country have global consequences.

3. **The birth of new socio-economic communities in various parts of the world is likely to dominate the landscape of the new renaissance in the twenty first century.** New networks and alliances, new patterns of trade, new methods of micro-financing are changing the landscape and emerging economies are playing an increasingly significant role in our politics and our economic life.

4. **Demographics are changing in such a way as to require:**

   - western economies to focus on innovation, immigration and productivity so as to sustain their societies

   - emerging economies to focus on value creation to develop their economies.

   There is and will continue to be a global war for talent.

5. **Core drivers of our communities – energy, water, climate and demographics – are changing in such a way as to make significant change inevitable.** Fewer and fewer people comprehend either the scale of these changes, their impact or their implications for the leadership of organizations, communities and nations.

6. **In the knowledge economy leadership development is one of the highest forms of leverage for an individual, an organization or a nation.** Leaders at all levels are faced with tasks that:

   - are challenging and for which their previous experiences have not fully prepared them

   - are complex and often ambiguous

   - do not necessarily lend themselves to conventional responses

- require collaboration among various stakeholders (internal and external)
- require both social and technological innovations
- often require the introduction of new information and communication technologies.

For over two decades, members of the *Innovation Expedition* have been exploring the key ideas which inform the ideas behind this book. The *Innovation Expedition* is a virtual global network organization. Drawing on a diverse community of affiliates, it serves as a great global connector—linking and supporting influential innovators and potential innovators in their efforts to build high performing organizations and to help create sustainable prosperity in their communities (jobs, wealth and well-being).

Our work on this book has been helped by comments, contributions and insights from a variety of members of this network. In particular, Jan Simpson (Redoaks Consulting), Bernadette Conraths (WHU, Koblenz), Matthias Kipping (Schulich Business School, York University), David Forrest and Keith Jones (Innovation Expedition Consulting Ltd.) have made many helpful suggestions. Susan Wasson and Michele Baker have also provided invaluable practical support. We especially want to acknowledge the substantive work of Jan Simpson in this context. Jan is a skilled writer in her own right and has substantial expertise in strategic communication. She did much to give shape to the sections of the book which focus on the characteristics of renaissance leaders.

A great deal of the thinking outlined in this book has been tried and tested with our clients in Europe, North America, Africa and Asia over the last decade. In particular, teaching at the Said Business School at Oxford University and on the Executive MBA at Athabasca University has tested this thinking thoroughly, as also has our work in many Fortune 500 companies.

This is the first in a series of books and resources describing our work. A second volume, focusing on implications of this work for health, education, business and other sectors will appear shortly. Also, a leadership development program associated with this thinking and offered through action learning, e-learning and engaged conversations is planned for 2010.

The book is in two parts. The first part, presented in Chapter 1 through 2, outlines a context for leadership in the twenty first century and the second part, from chapters 3 to 9 details the characteristics of renaissance leadership in some depth. The final chapters look at how this model of leadership connects to and complement other leadership frameworks and how we intend to use these concepts to drive leadership programs and developments in the future.

We have always said that "you cannot cross a chasm in two small leaps" – but it certainly helps to know how wide the chasm is before you jump!

Our hope for this book is that it provides a basis for looking in a systematic way at renaissance leadership in the context of a global knowledge economy that is changing and developing at a rapid pace.

Stephen Murgatroyd, PhD and D. G. Simpson, PhD
For the Innovation Expedition
February 2010

Chapter 1: The New Renaissance

Why Renaissance?

The term "renaissance" has an interesting history. It was not until the nineteenth century that the French word *"renaissance"* achieved popularity in describing the various cultural movements that began in the 13th century. It was first used in this way by the French historian Jules Michelet in 1855 and was made popular by the work of Jacob Burckhardt (1818-1897), especially with his book *The Civilization of the Renaissance in Italy* which, though originally published in 1860, remains a classic description of the Italian renaissance 1350-1550.

During the medieval renaissance, people found the courage to:

- Challenge generally accepted boundaries of thought and behaviour
- Explore and discover new areas – physically, mentally, artistically
- Question long held beliefs and traditional organizational structures – political, religious, social, artistic
- Develop a different and broader vision of themselves
- Create new ways of expressing themselves, of describing the world and of addressing the challenges faced by that world

- and these developments signified a shift from one world order to another – the renaissance was a "tipping point".

In this book, we are using the term "renaissance" as a powerful rallying call for creative change in periods of major paradigm shifts. We want to identify and support those leaders who are moved to action by awareness of the lessons from earlier renaissance periods and by a desire to emulate the behaviour of some of these leadership heroes from an earlier age.

The world has seen many "renaissances"—literally periods of rebirth, rejuvenation or reawakening in which a spirit of courageous, creative, open inquiry inspires breakthroughs in the arts, sciences, technology and business. This type of leadership in periods of major change ultimately leads to fundamental changes to economic, political and social models. Our thinking draws particularly on lessons from an iconic historical Renaissance in Europe and uses them to inspire modern day Renaissance leadership - but we are mindful that renaissances have occurred and continue to occur in many non European environments. We need to draw on these experiences also to influence our thinking and actions.

One renaissance figure many are familiar with is Leonardo da Vinci. He was a polymath, interested in many aspects of the world – science, engineering, art, music, botany, architecture, mathematics. He made his early living through music and his later living through art. He was curious about everything around him and his curiosity led him to systematic inquiry. He was engaged in the active pursuit of his interests. He did not just imagine or think about things, he did them. For him, there was only a small thinking-doing gap. Finally, he used all of his senses as a way of deepening his sensitivity to the world around him and as a means of sharpening his responses to that world. De Vinci was a renaissance man.

A modern renaissance man was Peter Drucker, who died in 2005 after a glorious career as a business educator and writer. His thirty-nine books written between 1939 and his death, together with his many public lectures and seminars show us, as Jeffrey Krames observes in his book *Inside Drucker's Brain*, that he was "the ultimate renaissance man". Drucker showed great interest in the early work of the Innovation Expedition aimed at strengthening the nonprofit sector. He honoured us by loaning us his most powerful brand (his name) and challenged us to identify, inspire, and celebrate outstanding leadership in Canadian nonprofits. We did this for 12 years through the Peter

F. Drucker Foundation for Non Profit Innovation, led by our colleague Dawn Ralph.

Peter Drucker provides the starting text for our view of the modern renaissance. He observed: "we are now in another critical moment: the transition from the industrial to the knowledge economy. We should expect radical changes in society as well as in business". Through our work on Renaissance Leadership we continue to utilize and celebrate what Peter taught us and we commit ourselves to introduce this amazing human being to a new generation of young leaders who do not know him.

The modern view of "renaissance" is that it refers not to a particular time in history or events in a particular location but to a series of events, some of which are contradictory or paradoxical. It refers to significant and irreversible change in the way society views art, itself and others and how individuals relate to each other. Also involved is a change in the role of institutions and a different role for science and religion. In short – it's a description of a period of flux in which some of the fundamentals of society change.

Characteristics of the "Old" Renaissance

The world has seen many "renaissances". Many regions can be seen to fit this description—England, Germany, France, Spain, Netherlands, Poland and many eastern European countries claim a renaissance. They each experienced different events, influences and changes, but common to them are these seven elements:

1. Changes in understanding of the nature of a nation state and the way in which its citizens relate to it.

2. A revival of an interest in the past. In the medieval period, this focused on antiquity and the lessons that could be learned from a better understanding of antiquity.

3. A strong and abiding interest in science and technology.

4. Changes in the patterns of trade and commerce, bringing with it new understandings of the world and the "way the world works" — especially in terms of cultural differences.

5. An understanding of the importance of the arts (painting, sculpture, theatre, literature, design) in shaping communities and its leaders.

6. The emergence of new institutions and new alliances.

7. A changed view of the way in which man relates to nature — largely informed by advances in scientific thinking and philosophy.

The idea of a renaissance is about a focus on changes in world-view and meaning, rather than just events in a particular location over a particular time.

A Modern Day Renaissance

We are living through a renaissance period now. Whether in North America, Europe, China, India, Brazil or the United Arab Emirates, this is a different time from that in these same places in the 1970's and 1980's.

In the early 1960s the original thinker named Peter F. Drucker wrote down and published what a small core of perceptive leaders were already talking about: the idea that the emergence of knowledge as a key economic resource was beginning to spark a period of fundamental change around the globe.

Fast-forward from there to 2008, and see how the authoritative but often dusty tomes of *Encyclopedia Britannica* have ceded the field to an upstart, free compendium of knowledge called Wikipedia — written collaboratively by anyone with an Internet connection and a desire to contribute. It has more than 75,000 active contributors, working on more than 10 million articles in more than 150 languages, and is used by at least 684 million visitors around the world each year. This demonstrates a major shift in how we create, collect, store and access knowledge.

Clearly, we are living through another historical period of major changes. We are throwing off the shackles of the Industrial Era, with its mechanical models, strict hierarchies, division of labour into silos, and command-and-control leadership and exploring the appropriate operating principles for the global knowledge economy.

A highly educated populace is questioning authority, ignoring classical boundaries and collaborating freely, exploring innovative economic models, and demanding change from established institutions. One safe assumption behind all our efforts to support the development of Renaissance Leaders is that we are living through a new swing point in history. The new age began somewhere around 1970 with the coming together of a host of new realities (social and cultural, technological, economical, ecological, and political).

Some of the key drivers of change for this new era are:
- **great increase in global competition**—at the end of World War II, North America's economy was the only one not badly hurt by the war. Now the competition is global. The re-building of Europe and Japan was followed by amazing developments among the Asian "Tigers" (Thailand, Malaysia, Korea and others), and more recently by the BRIC countries (Brazil, Russia, India and China). Now competition is clearly global.
- **changing nature of competition**—competition is no longer dependent primarily on cheap electricity and raw materials. It is now more dependent on an educated workforce, an infrastructure for organizing and sharing information and entrepreneurial leaders with a capacity to motivate, integrate, collaborate and inspire others.
- **explosion of new technologies**—particularly information and communication technologies (computerization,

miniaturization, digitization, satellite communication, fibre optics and the Internet).

- **the emergence of global capital markets**—this is a dramatic change (made possible by the new communication technologies). This change is not high in the consciousness of most people but it led to a dramatic shift in the way business is conducted, to the globalization of business and to a significant shift in the nature and extent of competition.
- **dramatic change in demographic patterns**—both in terms of the aging of population and the shift in major population growth from developed to the developing countries.

An increasingly common description for this new age is "the global, highly competitive, fast changing knowledge-based economy". The arrival of this new economy has sparked a global, organizational revolution over the past quarter century. The world emerging from this revolution is unlike any known before. No longer are the key assets for business only the classical ones of raw materials and cheap labour. Most of the old criteria for organizational success have been turned upside down. Now key assets are a well-educated workforce, knowledge and the entrepreneurial, collaborative and innovative leadership to utilize this knowledge.

Policy-makers and business organizations throughout the world now find themselves in the position of needing to:
- figure out the new kind of economic game we are playing; understand the rules of this new game;
- develop the strategies and skills that will allow them to function successfully in the fast-changing game; and
- get themselves in condition to play the game energetically and enthusiastically.

These kinds of new economic challenges are not simply a problem to be faced by companies relying on international trade. They affect all firms, in any country, as the "playing field" is now global, and is based on knowledge as a critical resource. More importantly, it directly affects many other aspects of our lives—our health care and education systems, our social services, and our arts and culture activities all depend on the revenue obtained from the income of the market sector. Only nations that continue to create new wealth can sustain high-quality physical, social and cultural environments.

Signs and Signals of a New Renaissance

If the previous sections described the drivers of change, what then are the signs and signals that a modern day Renaissance is indeed underway? We are seeing:

Fundamental change in how people define and relate to their community: The emergence of social networks driven by like-minded individuals and groups linked by technology is redefining our notions of community and involvement. Blogs (web documents created instantly by anyone) are becoming focal points for news and information. Facebook, LinkedIn and MySpace connect millions of people with shared interests across time and space. YouTube is the new television, and iPods the vehicles for music sharing across boundaries. The ubiquitous cell phone is giving personal interconnectivity a new meaning. Specialized communities to create new goods and services can be established in seconds and begin transactions in minutes.

Artifacts that symbolize a changed understanding of the world: Art, music, architecture, texts, three-dimensional sculptures, and historiographies are all appearing which represent cross-cultural, inter-generational thinking—symbolizing the "flattening" of the world through instant communication. In Dubai, the world's first continually shape-shifting apartment building has been designed—changing our very notion of a building, and demonstrating the power of imagination combined with the ability to create incredibly complex technology.

Challenging of taken-for-granted assumptions and orthodoxy in general – and especially in science, technology, and nature: The ability to manipulate genes to change the structure of matter and the nature of plants; learning how to clone living things and grow embryos; the capacity to predict biological development, including individual susceptibility to specific illnesses—all these challenge our assumptions about the relationships between science and development and science and society.

Shifts in the geographic locus of knowledge and power: Dubai and Qatar are fast becoming the new financial centres for certain kinds of financial services. Qatar is the fastest growing economy in the world. Brazil, Russia, India, and China—the so-called BRIC economies—are fast emerging as new economic engines in the world economy and starting to challenge the established G8 economies. As they do so, the locus of economic power is shifting. Mumbai is an established innovation centre for technology in the same way that regions in the Middle East (especially the UAE, Kuwait, and Qatar) and China are emerging as leaders of green technology innovation in practice. Singapore is leading in stem cell biology; Silicon Valley in software development. More of these centres of excellence will emerge over the next 25 years, few of them located near the current centres of power. The geography of innovation is changing.

New gatekeepers of knowledge-authority and a global leveling of the playing field: Universities used to be the keepers of knowledge and the cradle of knowledge development. Increasingly, people are looking to new knowledge networks— clusters and networked centres of excellence and corporate academies—for ideas and innovation. Innovation is flowing rapidly across boundaries. The role of private capital in fostering innovation and knowledge development is becoming more critical.

The world is changing quickly. We hold that the emerging renaissance cannot be undone. History shows us once the dynamics of a renaissance have taken hold, there can be no turning back of the clock. The patterns that will shape power, knowledge, culture, economy, society for the next hundred years are being set right now.

Renaissance Cities

The early enabling environment for nurturing and supporting the emergence and testing of new ideas in the early Italian Renaissance was centered in a few outstanding cities. Florence provided the cradle for this rebirth but by the early 16th century, Venice and Rome had emulated this energy and became its equal. Throughout the 16th century the innovations born in these cities were slowly spreading throughout the rest of Europe. Erasmus of Rotterdam not only nurtured the movement in northern Europe, he came to be recognized as the eminent thinker and scholar of his time.

Three billion people currently live in cities. Some nineteen cities in the world are home to 10 million people or more – the Tokyo/Yokohama urban region, for example, is home to 33 million people (more than the population of Canada). Of the fifty largest cities in the world in 2008, ten are in Asia, seven in each of China, India, Europe and South America and six are in North America with three in the African continent. By 2015, there are likely to be 59 African cities with populations between 1 million and 5 million, 65 such cities in Latin America and the Caribbean, and 253 in Asia.

Large cities develop only where there are successful economies or high concentrations of political power. Within Africa, Asia, and Latin America, the largest cities are concentrated in the largest economies: Brazil and Mexico in Latin America, and China, India, Indonesia, and the Republic of Korea in Asia. In

1990 these nations contained all but one of the mega-cities of 1-5 million people or more. Despite the speed of change in urban populations, there is a (perhaps surprising) continuity in the location of important urban centres. Most of the largest urban centres in Latin America, Asia, Europe and North Africa today have been important urban centres for centuries.

But what are the characteristics of a renaissance city? Several leading urban planners and researchers are exploring this question and a model is emerging of the characteristics of a renaissance city. When we look at what these cities consider as a renaissance city, we see these characteristics:

1. **The City should be a centre for global mobility** – it should be a "go to" and "stay" destination for people who have highly qualified backgrounds and skills who are able to adapt to the culture and environment of the City and there is a fast track recognition of their foreign credentials. The city needs appropriate socio-cultural infrastructure (health care, education, culture, and social services) to retain highly qualified people.

2. **The City should be a transportation hub** – the City needs to be the centre for supply chain and distribution systems through effective road, rail and air transportation. Being an "aerotropolis" (having core air services and supportive air industries) is especially important for the rapid and global distribution of goods.

3. **The City should have a vibrant creative community** – the City needs to foster innovation and creativity in all areas of its activity, from public service through the arts and education and through its encouragement of creative forums.

4. **The City should systematically encourage entrepreneurship and the growth of enterprise** – The City should be business friendly and an advocate for business growth and development. It should support the incubation of enterprise, enable entrepreneurial activity,

encourage innovation and celebrate entrepreneurial achievement.

5. **The City Should Secure Its Talent Base and Encourage The Development and Deployment of Best Practices** – using global intelligence and other benchmarking practices, the City should seek to model best practice and be a major contributor to best practices globally. By becoming a leading city in the world for good governance and best practice in a range of sectors (education, health, policing, business), the City should actively seek to retain its talented people. A strong social infrastructure, effective policing and a sustained and vibrant arts and cultural community are also essential ingredients of talent retention.

6. **The City should Think Globally and Act Locally** – in each area that the City operates and supports, it needs to understand the global context and global developments and find a way to take appropriate action locally. For example, US cities have committed to climate change initiatives on a scale equivalent to what would have been the US Kyoto commitment if the US had signed the agreement. By understanding global conditions and acting locally, Cities lead the US in terms of a response to climate change.

Renaissance Organizations

In the renaissance world of the 21st Century, we need to understand the complex challenges facing organizations and the characteristics of organizations that will survive and thrive in this environment.

The central concepts that inform our thinking of what we might describe as Renaissance Organizations are these:

Knowledge based organizations that create discernable value and which are anchored in communities will dominate their sector. This is because the key to their success is sustained value creation and the commitment of people.

While brand matters, what matters more is the commitment of people within the organization to its future. It is clear that the best predictor of success in any organization is employee satisfaction.

Consumer behaviour will change, as will the dynamics of markets and the values that inform market behaviour, reflecting the rebalancing of the world economy and the emergence of strong new economies in diverse and unexpected locations throughout the world in the next 50 years.

Managing and balancing the dynamic relationship between a number of different forms of capital will be the key task of leadership in modern day Renaissance organizations:

> **Intellectual capital**—the power of people, their knowledge and their ability to learn quickly and broadly
>
> **Structural capital**—the power of processes, structure, best practices and styles of working which stay with the organization even when individuals leave
>
> **Customer capital**—the loyalty relationship with clients and customers which is the engine for profitability and performance
>
> **Agility capital**—responsiveness, speed and nimbleness including an agile learning ability
>
> **Collaborative capital**—the ability to help diverse stakeholders to focus, collaborate and innovate in order to address complex tasks; when action occurs, everyone is singing the same song to the same tune at the same time
>
> **Inspirational capital**—the task within the organization of enabling, encouraging and empowering performance
>
> **Performance capital**—focusing on actions which can be measured and understood within the organization and which address is its strategic direction

- finding the balance between the competing demands of these different forms of capital and doing so in a way that supports high performance is a major challenge for renaissance leaders.

A renaissance organization is an organization that is aware of the renaissance shifts taking place within and around them and that is able to leverage these changes to their advantage. These are the organizations that do more than survive in this renaissance age – they thrive and prosper. They lead the sector in which they are part and do so deliberately and by choice. As organizations, they are seen as renaissance leaders.

The Importance of Knowledge in the Global Economy

Peter Drucker credits a Princeton economist, Fritz Machlup with the first use of the term "Knowledge Industries" in his 1962 book, *Production and Distributional Knowledge in the United States*. If Drucker was not the first to coin the phrase, he certainly was the leader in popularizing and explaining the concept and in applying it, not just to individual industries but to society as a whole.

He suggested that the emergence of knowledge as a key economic resource would be one of the forces that would spark a historic period of fundamental change which we are now describing as a Modern-Day Renaissance.

Since 1968, there has been an increasing, although vague, recognition of the economic value of knowledge. Many calls are made for increased investments in knowledge, but the qualitative measurement of knowledge is an elusive art.

Some of the beneficial consequences of increased investments in knowledge are seen to be:

- faster product innovation;
- better tailoring through technology of customized customer service;
- joint innovation with customers of new opportunities;
- improved product quality; and
- empowered ways of providing customer service.

These are the returns on knowledge investment. Yet many are still struggling to understand the nature of the investment, how to treat knowledge as an economic resource, and how to improve the performance of knowledge workers.

We suggest that a useful starting point for understanding the changing nature of knowledge is to consider that we now need to become literate in a number of different types of knowledge.

In the knowledge economy and the knowledge driven organization we are not just concerned with having knowledge about various technical and scientific issues—we are now grappling with understanding how to connect with people who have key knowledge, how to integrate and successfully apply knowledge to achieve a purpose and how we develop knowledge about knowledge itself. We can speak of at least six distinctly different types of knowledge in which we need to be literate and leverage knowledge:

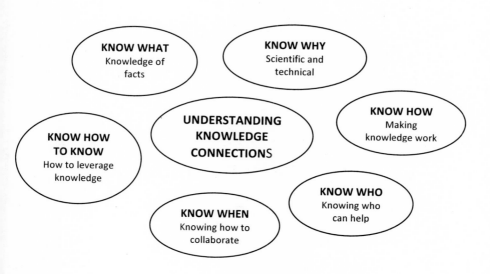

By understanding each of these knowledge domains, leveraging them effectively and building teams which can make use of these different knowledge forms, organizations can build distinct, sustainable competitive advantage.

The question that follows is: what kind of leadership can act on these characteristics and these forms of knowledge in a way that helps that organization become and stay a renaissance organization? How do leaders need to think, see, act and engage others so as to build and sustain a renaissance organization? This is the focus of the balance of this book.

Chapter 2: The Leadership Challenges of the New Renaissance

Imagine these six challenges being on your desk on your first day in a leadership role of an organization:

- A global supply chain is blocked because of water shortages in a particular production location in Canada, caused by global warming. The only two other suppliers of this core component for one of your best selling products currently supply the competition – one is located in Russia and the other in Venezuela.
- Key information required to manage an organization has been stolen by persons unknown from a country unknown. Some 32,000 client files may be compromised. This is the second time such a breach has occurred in the last twenty four months.
- A competitor, working from a manufacturing base in India, has developed a breakthrough version of a key product which provided your company with 22% of its revenues for the last five years – the competitor will be able to undercut your price, quickly take market share and provide a more reliable product which better meets customer requirements.
- Climate change regulations will have a negative impact on profitability and performance for your organization.
- Your HR director has just completed their HR capacity forecast for the next five years. It shows that for each of the next four years, 37% of the workforce is scheduled to retire. To grow the business in line with the business plan requires an annual growth of 14% in staff – annually, the organization needs to recruit the equivalent of 30% of its staff and retain all others. About 20% of the staff required need specialist skills which are in short supply globally.
- New research suggests that the five products which generate 80% of your company's income could be

seriously impacted by emerging technologies now being developed in China, USA and Russia.

Each of these are real situations– fortunately, they are not all on the desk of the same leader in the same organization at the same time. The point: organizations are affected by the kind of changes described in the last chapter. Whether it is the war for talent, the emergence of new sciences and technologies, climate change, technology dependency or being able to leverage jurisdictional advantage, there are significant challenges faced daily by leaders at all levels in an organization which result from the new world.

The leaders of nonprofit organizations also face challenges, as do those working in government or related organizations. These include (but are not limited to):

- Challenge of securing and retaining highly qualified people.
- Making sense of rapidly changing social and political circumstances where communication is instant, complex and uncertain.
- Leveraging technology in the service of the organization.
- Developing knowledge and understanding relevant to the challenges faced by the organization, yet protecting this knowledge in appropriate ways.
- Making sense of the new social networks which are driving civil society and determining how best to communicate by means of these networks.
- Re-engaging individuals with the work of politics, looking beyond the short term and focusing on medium to long-term.
- Securing public funding for activities which are increasingly seen as "niche" or marginal by politicians – an especial issue for nonprofit arts organizations.
- Managing the flow of information against competing sources of intelligence.

- It is not easy being a leader in a twenty first century organization of any kind.

Whether the organization is for profit or not for profit, "the future isn't what it used to be" (Yogi Berra). Each organization needs a new level of nimble absorption – an ability to quickly absorb new ideas and developments and leverage them to their advantage. Innovation is no longer an option for most organizations, it is a description of a core behavior which will enable them to prosper and grow.

The challenges a modern organization faces are:
- Increasingly complex
- Often highly ambiguous
- Stretching leaders beyond their comfort zones and well past their education and training
- Demanding of leaders – requiring them to rethink their approaches and their understanding of how the world now functions

To deal with the kind of challenges we have just outlined, organizations need renaissance leaders – individuals who can think, understand, act and change in a way that commands followership.

Understanding the Context of 21st Century Leadership

The W. K. Kellogg Foundation has been engaged in scanning activities with respect to leadership for the twenty first century. Using literature reviews, interviews, surveys, they have been exploring the question: What does leadership need to be like for the new century?

Data from this work consistently point to the notion that leadership is a means to an end, not an end in and of itself. Answering the question "leadership for what?" requires thoughtful consideration that any evaluation of effective leadership be inextricably linked to analysis of outcomes. Effective leadership is moving from hierarchical, top-down leadership models to inclusive, participatory leadership styles. Effective individual leaders are people who commit themselves to tackling challenges, help their organization and their community articulate a vision for change, and build the commitment and wherewithal to improve the lives of people within the organization and community.

These scans provide insight into current thinking about what attributes, knowledge, and skills leaders should possess to ensure their effectiveness in a global, knowledge-based, multicultural society. Future leaders, like their predecessors, must have a deep sense of mission and passion guided by strong moral, ethical, and spiritual values. Organizations and communities want leaders to reflect their vision and values for positive social change and to display courage and determination to achieve this vision.

Effective leaders are humble, self-aware, and have a high degree of accountability. They believe in the need for many people to have a seat at the table, and recognize the importance of diverse perspectives and skills. Through inclusion and charisma, they inspire confidence among many and are able to raise the level of motivation and morality among a group to help find solutions and ensure progress.

Scan respondents to the W. K. Kellogg surveys indicated that effective leaders must be open to change and capable of a long-term vision and a culturally sensitive world perspective. This requires continuous learning and personal development. As Shimon Peres, President of Israel, commented in an interview, leaders need to continue to learn so that they are "up to tomorrow," rather than just "up to date." He echoes the famous Wayne Gretzky quote – "you don't just need to know where the puck is, you need to know where it's going to be".

Unlike any previous time in our history, it is essential that leaders have the ability to master new technologies, and in particular, developments in information technology. Knowing how to capitalize on the advantages of evolving communications systems is essential. As Frances Hesselbein from the Peter F.

Drucker Foundation remarked in an interview, "the globalization of ideas is far more powerful than the globalization of business." Information and knowledge are replacing physical resources as the most important currency in the world. Great leaders of the future will be good interpretive thinkers who know how to look at both the big picture and the micro vision and propose realistic solutions. They must be able to help their organizations and the communities in which they operate, comprehend and act on complex interconnected issues and problems with intelligence, creativity, and good judgment.

The leaders of the future must have confidence and excellent management skills. Leaders must recognize their strengths and weaknesses and know how to build complementary teams. They should be capable of developing collaborative working relationships across numerous and varied constituencies and stakeholders. They should feel comfortable operating at all levels of society to affect and institutionalize change. Partnerships and strategic alliances are critical for effective leadership; the new leader must know how to network and build coalitions to get things done.

Looking beyond their own sector and immediate sphere of influence, leaders must know how to work with the others, whether it is corporate, government, or NGOs, because the complexity of modern problems requires that the three sectors combine resources and influence to forge new solutions. Just look at climate change management for examples of such collaboration.

Finally, the leaders of the 21st century must have a global perspective and be willing to embrace diversity and cultural differences. Contextual demands on our leaders will require that they use a wide-angle lens and look beyond immediate boundaries and borders to solve problems. Effective leaders will encourage multiple viewpoints and will be comfortable with sharing leadership. They will know how to identify and nurture emerging leaders among them. New leaders must teach the importance of tolerance and compassion and must help people learn how to live together.

Renaissance Leaders are Different

We have just described the core conditions for effective and inspiring leadership for the twenty first century organizations. But this description is general – it speaks to the necessary conditions for effective leadership.

These conditions are necessary, but not sufficient for renaissance leaders. As you will see in the subsequent chapters of this book, renaissance leaders need to go beyond these necessary conditions and practice six specific skills on a systematic and regular basis for effective renaissance leadership. What kind of leadership will offer the greatest chance in this fast changing world of harnessing the creative energy required to drive dramatic improvements in organizational performance, deliver harmonious prosperity and desirable quality of life for everyone in one's own community and in others around the globe? We believe it's a style of leadership we call Renaissance Leadership.

Renaissance Leaders aren't easily described in a few neat phrases, precisely because they embody the Renaissance tendency to break down rigid categories and wander into areas where the Industrial mind would say they had no right to be.

Consider Leonardo da Vinci, a name often invoked as the quintessential Renaissance Man. Was he a scientist, mathematician, engineer, inventor, anatomist, painter, sculptor, architect, botanist, musician, or writer? Exactly.

Or Cosimo de Medici: ambassador, politician, patron of arts and architecture, banker and businessman, founder of a modern Platonic philosophical academy – and one of the lead players in the 15th century Italian Renaissance.

The Renaissance Leaders were thinkers—but not the type of thinker who prefers the ivory tower and indulges in thought purely for its own sake. They were thinkers with a passion for moving their ideas and knowledge to action.

In a similar way Renaissance Leaders in the modern knowledge economy are also people of action—but not the ready-fire-aim type of actor who believes that being fast off the mark in implementing the first plan that comes to mind is the key to success. They are self-aware people who pay attention to who they really are – what some might call their "way of being in the world"—without descending into self-absorption or losing touch with reality.

They are high integrity individuals with a passion both for driving high performance in their organizations and for helping to make the world a better place.

These modern day Renaissance leaders have a sense of history and an unusual capacity for viewing the world holistically, for practicing systems thinking, for injecting a global and a futures perspective into present challenges, for honouring diversity, and for drawing on ideas and best practices from diverse disciplines and economic sectors.

They have a capacity to function as social and technical architects designing new structures, processes and products for addressing complex challenges.

They have mastered the art of demonstrating grace under pressure, and of inspiring others to have the courage to collaborate and innovate in order to solve complex challenges.

This is because renaissance leaders are role models for other leaders – they have moved from being a good leader to a great leader who inspires others to lead their organizations and communities differently. Renaissance leaders understand the future and know how they need to lead to make the future a positive one for their organization.

Renaissance Leaders Collaborate

Renaissance leaders collaborate – they understand that collaboration is the DNA of the knowledge economy. They also understand the range and scope of the collaboration required to build an effective, focused renaissance organization. They seek out:

Collaboration Among People Who Work in the Same Department

Because changes are taking place in several areas, all of which are interrelated, there is a need for collaboration. This is particularly true because leaders are expected to deal with these issues holistically, which means dealing with all of the above issues in some integrated fashion.

Collaboration Among Different Departments of the Same Organization

Since changes in organizations play themselves out in at least five functional areas of work (Strategy, Structure, Systems, Skills, and Shared Values), there is an increasing need for collaboration among people from different parts of the organization.

Collaboration in Cross Functional Virtual Teams to Run Specific Projects

An elaboration of these two forms of collaboration reminds us that increasingly organizations need to put together cross-functional teams to undertake a specific task. These people come together from various parts of the company in what is usually a short term or part-time secondment. Often the secondment is informal.

This collaboration requires a mixed group to learn how to work together efficiently and effectively quickly and when the task is completed they go back to their old department and a new collaborative team is formed to tackle a new task.

Collaboration of Organization with its Suppliers or Customers

In the global knowledge economy, increasingly organizations concentrate on their key competencies which allow them to add high value and work out collaborative relationships with others who have high competencies in areas needed by them. In some cases this involves collaboration with their suppliers and/or customers. In other cases, another company may at one moment be your customer; at another moment your supplier;

and at another moment your partner in designing a new product. Collaboration is dynamic and adaptive.

Collaboration with Other Competitors in your Sector (the concept of Strategic Alliances) - the building of effective clusters

Strategic alliances began in Europe in the late 1970s and early 1980s and represented an attempt by several firms in the electronic sector to save themselves from Japanese competitors during a time when the European economies were being described as sick (suffering from *"Eurosclerosis"*, as one writer suggested*)*. The evolving response to this crisis was to find an efficient and effective way to collaborate with former competitors to run significant projects or create a new product without having to create a merged new company or a legal joint venture.

Organizations cooperated to a certain point then took the results back to their own organization and competed. Having learned how to organize alliances with former competitors in Europe, some firms gained the confidence to explore similar alliances with the "enemy" companies from Asia. This concept of flexible strategic alliances found its way into various sectors and a new range of operating principles and leadership skills emerged to support such collaborative initiatives.

Public Good Collaboration Among Different Sectors of Society (for Profit, Non-profit, Public)

There is a need to help people see that concept of a Collaborative Culture is not just a nice thing now. It has become critical for our economic success and our social wellbeing. Many profit making companies are now seeing this collaboration as being essential for maintaining quality of life in their community which is essential for the economic well being of the company and for its ability to attract top level employees.

Also this collaboration offers employees of for-profit companies great opportunities to develop badly needed leadership skills (team building, relationship building, etc.) and offers their employees opportunity to build citizenship skills—companies can't do it easily. Government is withdrawing from this area.

This area of collaboration offers government agencies opportunities to build new relationships with profit making and nonprofit groups and develop the agencies capacity to add value that is not just dependent upon handing out money.

New Collaborative Roles Between Employer and Employee

The new realities of a fast changing, highly competitive global knowledge economy has put severe new pressures on the conventional long term employee/employer relationship.

It is now more difficult for employers to offer secure long term employment, yet more than ever they need a commitment from employees to work as if the business was their own business. Also, the reliance on knowledge as a key competitive asset means that employers need to constantly find new knowledge workers and retain the commitment of those whose knowledge is critical for their present success.

All this has led to new tensions between employer and their knowledge workers and has begun to inspire the creation of quite different collaborative arrangements between them.

Collaboration is no longer a "soft", HR related idea – it's a driver for competitive advantage. Renaissance leaders understand this and actively model collaborative behaviour.

Renaissance Leaders Know How to Focus and Then Unleash Innovation

There is growing recognition of the important role of agile learning and collaboration linked to the systematic and focused work of the organization as an innovator. In our understanding, innovation is a discipline that can be taught—and learned—and that the way one structures an organization can either support innovation or impede it. Organizations need to focus on recognizing that innovation is more than research—more than just a good idea. It is a good idea *that has been made to work*. That is, innovation involves a complex process that leads to a product or service that either meets a demand or creates one.

Meeting or creating demand requires a supply chain that involves commercial practices and effective management.

When we look at innovation as a focused, systematic organizational practice, we see different types of innovation. These include:

- technological and social innovations
- incremental and breakthrough innovations
- innovations in strategy, structure, support systems, skills and shared values
- innovation at the individual, organizational or inter-organizational level
- innovations in products and services
- process innovations (changing the way work is undertaken)
- innovations in culture (changing the organizational structure and the operating principles including changing attitudes and behaviours)

To be effective, these innovations need to be:

- an executed idea—something that's gone from drawing board to implementation
- an idea which has sustainable value—it lasts for more than a day or so as measured by performance improvements over time
- something that makes a difference that people are willing to pay for, either directly (through price) or indirectly (by demanding the service) or which reduces costs.

Innovation can involve completely new developments—as in a "breakthrough" which changes the way we do things—such as the development of the internet which has changed the nature of commerce, created new opportunities for learning systems and spawned new kinds of organizations. Or innovation can be an improvement on existing practices or technologies such as different ways of eliminating exhaust emissions from a car or a new way of extracting crude oil from the Alberta oil sands.

In our view, innovation is a mindset, disposition and skill set that can be taught and nurtured over time.

The Need for some Disciplined Thinking about Innovation

New innovation policies and practices are needed within organizations to respond to the different operating principles of a knowledge-based economy. Indeed, we are now looking at what is known as "third generation" innovation policies and practices:

- **First generation**—This understanding of innovation sees it as a linear process that is initiated by lab science (fundamental research) and moves through successive stages until the new knowledge is built into commercial applications that diffuse into the economic system. This outdated view of the innovation supply chain still seems to be dominant in many people's minds. The current dominant idea is that firm's contract with R&D labs, which produce ideas which then get commercialized.

- **Second generation**—This approach recognizes the complexity of the innovation system with many feedback loops between the different stages outlined in the first generation model, with products and services emerging from a web of interactions.

- **Third generation**—This approach views innovation as a more complex integrated process and places innovation at the heart of all policy areas shaping the performance of our economy (research, science and technology, education, competition, value-added strategy, regional policy, immigration, etc.). It also recognizes a critical starting point for innovation with a firm that has a client with a problem to be solved and then creating the mechanism by which the clients' needs can be met.

We need to avoid pitting the universities against firms and firms against each other within a region when refining innovation policies, either within an industry or within a region. We need to become more informed about and responsive to the appropriate balance of investments in skills, technologies, research, outsourced innovation and the process of identifying customer needs and opportunities.

Building a culture of innovation in any country thus requires a greater understanding of and respect for commerce among the populace and a clearer appreciation for what it takes to build globally competitive, innovative enterprises. A few years back we organized and implemented a national Dialogue on this topic of how to grow globally competitive, innovative enterprises. It was done for a Federal, Provincial, and Territorial Task Force. The sobering output from this Dialogue can be found in our Innovation Watch website (www.innovationwatch.com). As a result of this experience, we crafted a somewhat funky but serious Innovation Manifesto to help trigger collaborative out-of-the-box thinking and appropriate innovative actions among our team and our clients. Each organization needs its own version of an Innovation Manifesto.

Leading Organizations that Innovate, Collaborate and Perform

The balance of this book looks at the nature and skills of renaissance leadership and provides insight into these skills and their meaning. The intention: to provide an understanding of what it takes to lead and sustain a renaissance organization competing and performing in a knowledge driven economy.

Chapter 3: The Six Practices of Renaissance Leaders

Introduction

The Innovation Expedition has been working with leaders in government, for profit and non profit organizations across the world for over twenty years. We have leveraged this experience and that of our highly experienced network to ask the question: When we look at the "stand out" leaders of the current age – those who understand the new renaissance and are leading their organizations to be best in class – what do we see them doing?

The Six Practices

Our response is that there are a great many factors which shape effective leadership within a sector or organization, but that six key characteristics stand out as necessary conditions for renaissance leadership. We studied other leadership models, as you will see, and reviewed the thirty six dominant leadership competencies which we found dominated the literature. We reflected on what this meant for our view of leaders in these renaissance times. In our view, renaissance leaders:

Practice personal mastery

They have high integrity and view self-awareness as a prerequisite for leadership. They work hard to develop their capacity to innovate, and to inspire others to join them in making the world a better place.

Apply a glocal mindset

They have a keen sense of history and seek a holistic understanding of changes taking place on a global scale. They use this global perspective as they address local challenges and seize opportunities (global and local – hence "glocal").

Accelerate cross-boundary learning

They constantly seek to satisfy an intense curiosity about every facet of human life, past and present, scientific and artistic, technical and social. They guide others in distilling meaning from a morass of information, and efficiently apply their learning in creative ways to nurture innovation and drive improved performance.

Think back from the future

They are readily able to imagine and articulate alternate futures and work back from there – connecting with lessons from the past to better understand the present and choose among possible paths to the future they see.

Lead systemic change

They are systems thinkers who seek out patterns, inter-connections and interdependencies. They are skilled in seeking common ground and nurturing productive collaboration across diverse parts of a system – be it an organization, a sector, a community, a network – to solve complex problems and drive large-scale change.

Drive performance with a passion

They care that their leadership makes a substantive and sustainable difference, and are relentless in their commitment to performance. They articulate clear (and high) expectations of themselves and others, create focused strategies for innovating to achieve these ends, and are disciplined about assessing progress.

These six characteristics are not listed in order of importance nor are they intended to be complete – it is the list we have arrived at on this stage of our expedition.

The pages which follow provide more detail and examples of each of these six characteristics and suggest some activities which you can pursue to deepen your understanding of each of them. The intention is to lay out the terrain and suggest some map references which will ground your own journey to understanding the new renaissance and its emerging leaders.

These ideas were developed and refined through a series of workshops at the Saïd School of Business, Oxford with mature international leaders and has been refined in dialogue with many organizations and individuals since. Many have found this a powerful and effective starting point for a conversation about leadership in a twenty first century organization - exactly as we intended.

Some have observed that the key characteristics of renaissance leaders, as described in more detail in the balance of this book, are deceptively simple to list but difficult to practice daily. Others have suggested that keeping the list of six characteristics close to hand helps them be better leaders daily. Our intent, in offering this thinking, is to challenge you to think about a simple question: "What kind of leadership does a renaissance organization lead and how can the key characteristics of these leaders best be captured?"

Chapter 4: Personal Mastery

Introduction

Renaissance Leaders practice personal mastery: They have high integrity and view self-awareness as a prerequisite for leadership. They work hard to develop their capacity to innovate, and to inspire others to join them in making the world a better place. Here are some of the things that are indicative of the search for personal mastery:

Approaching life as artwork-in-progress: For aspiring leaders or students of organizations coming of age in North America in the 90s, the phrase "personal mastery" is indelibly associated with Peter Senge's seminal book, *The Fifth Discipline: The Art & Practice of the Learning Organization* – one of the five core disciplines essential to building organizations "where people continually expand their capacity to create the results they truly desire, where new and expansive patterns of thinking are developed and nurtured, where collective aspiration is set free, and where people are continually learning how to learn together."[1] For Senge, personal mastery goes beyond competence and skills, although it is grounded in competence and skills. It goes beyond spiritual unfolding or opening, although it requires spiritual growth. It means approaching one's life as a creative work – a work always in progress (page 141).

Making the analogy with a master craftsperson whose personal and professional proficiency enable the best pots or fabrics to emerge from the workshop, Senge describes personal mastery as a lifelong process of approaching life as an artist would approach a work of art. The keys are continually clarifying what's important to you, learning how to see current reality more

---

[1] Senge, p. 3. The other disciplines, in addition to personal mastery, are mental models, building shared vision, team learning – and the fifth discipline, systems thinking, that integrates them all.

clearly, and working with the forces of change to resolve the creative tension between your vision of what might be and where things are now.

People who practice personal mastery are acutely aware of their ignorance and their incompetence, but also deeply self-confident.

Asking the right questions to manage oneself: The notion that deep self-awareness is the foundation on which a leader's ability to act effectively in the world is not new. The admonition "know thyself" is said to have been carved onto the walls of the temple of Apollo at Delphi, greeting leaders coming to consult the Oracle on matters of war and state in ancient times. What is new, according to Peter Drucker, writing in the 1970s, is that to have even a chance of success and achievement in the new economy, knowledge workers need to learn to manage themselves. Until sometime in the mid 20th century, the norm was for people to be born into a line of work, and so knowing your strengths was irrelevant. If the peasant's son wasn't good at being a peasant, he failed.

Now people have choices. They have to discover what they're good at. Whereas through most of history, most people have been subordinates who did as they were told, knowledge workers must answer a new question: "What should my contribution be?" To successfully make that contribution, they must understand their personal mode of performance, and pay attention to the strengths, values, and performance modes of others:

Amazingly few people know how they get things done. On the contrary, most of us do not even know that different people work and perform differently. We therefore work in ways that are not our ways—and that almost guarantees non-performance.

Renaissance leaders, in addition to developing a sense of personal mastery, manage themselves – they are self-starters and capable of undertaking complex projects without losing their sense of self or being "taken over" by the projects and their demands – in the midst of complexity, renaissance leaders are an island of simplicity: they understand the complex, but can make clear and explicit what needs to be done, by whom, by when and they know what part they must play in making things happen. Knowing themselves and how they work best enables them to manage and support others.

Exploring diversity: There are, of course, many systems designed to help people appreciate such differences. One can trace a link from the work of the Greek doctor Hippocrates (460-370 BC) on how bodily fluids or "humours" (blood, yellow bile, black bile and phlegm) affected human behavior to the variations on the sanguine, choleric, melancholic and phlegmatic personality types described by 20th century psychologists. These days, people are most likely to explore the differences through tests based on the Myers-Briggs Type Indicator or the True Colors character cards.

Some may find themselves drawn to Peter Koestenbaum's Leadership Diamond Model. It's a three dimensional model for probing the mysteries of life and leadership by asking you to reflect on your fundamental orientation towards the world – your way of being intelligent: are you a visionary, a pragmatist, a people person, or an explorer?

Your fundamental mastery of the different modes of existence – your way of being competent: your mastery of greatness (maintaining excitement and hope), of polarity (managing uncertainty and coping with ambiguity), of resistance (your openness to the truth about yourself), of teaching (leading by helping others learn).

Your levels of depth (forms of enrichment) – your level of professional enrichment (personal or individual development), of social/cultural/ethnic enrichment (societal context and community), psychological enrichment (the unconscious as a source of both power and failure), and philosophical enrichment (questions of consciousness, spirituality).

The framework that Peter Senge found most useful is *Human Dynamics*, created by Dr. Sandra Seagal and David Horne. In the foreword to their 1997 book, he writes:

> *"One of the foundational strengths of Human Dynamics...is that the differences among the personality dynamics are truly a source of richness to be celebrated and appreciated, without <u>any</u> implicit judgment...the Human Dynamics approach is inherently developmental. Rather than sticking people in a box and saying, "This is how you are," it illuminates our distinctive patterns of growth and change. Each personality dynamic is seen as a whole system, evolving in particular ways...It leads to seeing each of us as a <u>process</u> rather than a <u>thing</u>."*

Human Dynamics is based on the premise that three fundamental aspects of human functioning combine in highly specific ways in people to form distinct patterns of functioning called "personality dynamics". These three patterns are shown below in Figure 1.

Mental	Thinking — Objectivity — Vision — Overview — Structure — Values
Emotional	Feeling — Subjectivity — Communication — Organization — Create Imagination
Physical	Making — Doing — Actualizing — Sensory Experience — Practicality — Systematic Experience

Figure 1: Patterns of Functioning

While the interaction of these three patterns (also referred to as principles) creates nine potential dynamics, five occur most commonly (see stories on following pages). Understanding these patterns gives us unique insights into how we—and others—experience our environment, process information, prefer to communicate, learn, problem-solve, relate to ourselves and others, maintain wellness and develop. Each type brings unique and essential gifts.

Human Dynamics seeks to "illuminate our different ways of functioning so we may make more efficient and enlightened use of ourselves." Just as important, we can also then work consciously to meet the needs of people with other personality dynamics, recognizing that "diversity is the intended purpose of nature – to be respected, celebrated, and utilized."

Human Dynamics' developmental thrust starts with understanding and fully realizing the gifts inherent in our foundational dynamic (the name of which reflects the two patterns with which we are most at home – mental, emotional, and physical). But the third pattern is always present in each of us, and the richer journey that so excited Senge is the development and integration of this third strand.

To illustrate the power of these ideas, here are some extracts of stories from five combinations of principle factors for five different people. As you read these, put yourself in the position of someone who works with them – what would be your challenges in working with this person?

Mental – Physical: "I am most attuned to the world of thoughts, vision, concepts, and overviews. I am easily able to maintain focus and can inspire that gift in others. I often bring structure, objectivity, and precision to projects and interactions...I seek to articulate overarching principles and values to which all can subscribe."

Emotional –Objective (Mental): "I am a problem-solver with an affinity for generating new ideas and promoting innovation. I relish change and challenge and am alert for windows of opportunity...striving to cultivate group synergy for the purpose of building something new and enduring that will benefit humankind.

Emotional – Subjective (Emotional): "All of my experiences are personalized. I have personal responses to everything, and want to connect personally with everything and everyone. I have a wide range of feelings and am sensitive to and interested in the feelings of others...I have a visionary capacity, which can enable me to be an inspirational communicator and an effective long-range 'seer.'"

Physical-Mental: "I am a natural systems thinker interested in concrete work. I want to translate thoughts and ideas into practical results that satisfy a need or solve a problem. I especially excel in the tactical implementation of work...Another deep purpose is to create unity out of diversity by maintaining bonds among all group members in the spirit of community."

Physical-Emotional: "I am practical, detailed, thorough, and precise. I am also a natural strategic planner and systems thinker. I have a strategy for almost everything I do. I tend to assemble and reassemble data until interconnected patterns or systems change...One of my deep purposes is to formulate and implement plans and activities that reflect a compassionate concern for the welfare of people and that answer a collective need."

While the creators of Human Dynamics seek to "lift the human spirit" in their work, the authors of *Why CEOs Fail* urge us to lift the taboo on exploring the "dark side," satisfying "our natural impulse to wonder about our negative impulses as leaders, to investigate why we take actions that hurt others, ourselves, and our organizations." Long in the business of training and coaching leaders, David Dotlich and Peter Cairo are fascinated by the question of why bright, savvy, highly experienced and talented business leaders with terrific track records act in illogical, idiosyncratic or irrational ways, sabotaging themselves and their companies. Starting from psychologist Robert Hogan's research on leadership "derailers," they explore 11 traits that, when well managed, are positive contributors to a leader's success, but can turn into serious derailers under conditions of stress.

Examples of Leadership Derailers

Here are six examples of the way in which the balance of the three principles can impair leadership performance:

- When self-confidence slides into arrogance, leaders become blind to how their actions are hurting themselves and their companies
- Charisma and an appropriate leader–like "presence" can become melodrama, detracting from other people's performances and impairing ability to see what's going on
- Prudent thoroughness turned into excessive caution and over analysis can result in a fatal failure to act decisively at the critical moment
- Healthy skepticism can become habitual distrust, leading employees to watch their backs rather than their work, and stop believing in themselves
- A willingness to challenge the status quo and redefine industries can degenerate into impulsive mischievousness and destructive rule breaking
- An appropriate perfectionism taken too far can mean the little things are put right while the big things go wrong

And so on. The book is written through the lens of the CEO because the authors believe that the vast majority of top executives don't receive adequate feedback or confrontation to help them understand their personalities and their impact they have on others or the organization as a whole. But leaders of any stripe can benefit from understanding their personal derailers, figuring out what kind of stress triggers them, and learning to manage these stressors proactively.

Seeking support

While personal mastery is by definition focused on an individual leader, it need not be solitary.

Most Renaissance Leaders seek help from others to maintain personal mastery – coaching, guidance, mentoring, as well as opportunities for challenges that will stretch their skills, network and imagination.

More and more, virtual networks are becoming part of the mix as people use technology to build a web of support and knowledge that can span the world. Blogs and shared bookmarking, member-driven news sites like diigo.com, popular social networks *My Space* and *Facebook*, professional networks such as LinkedIn – the Internet offers a wealth of opportunities for people to seek advice and specialized resources, learn and share learning.

Chapter 5: Applying a "Glocal" Mind Set

Introduction

The term "glocal" refers to the idea of understanding the global context in which local actions need to be taken and the impact local actions could have on global developments.

"The world is flat," proclaimed Thomas Friedman in 2005, more than 500 years after Christopher Columbus ostensibly championed the idea of a spherical earth to a skeptical world (in fact, the concept is at least as old as the ancient Greeks, and was generally accepted by scholars and navigators in 15th century Europe).

Friedman's world is flat in the sense that globalization has leveled the competitive playing fields between industrial and emerging market economies. The global web of information and communication technologies has made it possible for companies to locate call centers thousands of miles from the customers they support, outsource accounting and programming to offshore contractors, create complex global supply chains that take advantage of the most cost-effective sources of skilled labour wherever they may be located. The collapse of the Berlin wall and the end of the cold war marked the beginning of a new economic openness to the world on the part of countries like Brazil, India, China and Russia — countries that are now such significant players on the world markets that they have their own acronym: BRIC.

With competitive advantage now driven more by innovation — the creation and application of knowledge — than by availability of raw materials and cheap electricity, location matters less. While people are migrating from less-developed economies to fill the gap created by declining birth rates and aging populations in the more developed countries in North America and Europe, countries like India are putting their highly educated knowledge workers to work on virtual global teams without ever leaving home. Financial capital now flows freely around the globe.

Increased competition and shifting trade patterns are disrupting industries, and challenging key and established notions about statehood and economic boundaries.

Exploring the new world of the global knowledge economy

Renaissance Leaders understand that a new world has been emerging over the past four or five decades, and that navigating it will require fundamental adjustments to their mental maps. Just as physical maps of the world are influenced by one's biases – North American maps routinely put North America in the centre, even at the cost of splitting Asia in two, while Chinese maps clearly show "the middle kingdom" in its rightful place – so too do our assumptions about the way the world works influence what we are able to see. The resources in this book offer a starting point for a way of looking at our emerging, global knowledge economy.

Global management practice

While Drucker asserts that the global knowledge economy rests on foundations developed in the Western world – Western science, tools and technology, production, economics; Western-style finance and banking – Ronald Lessen as early as the late 80's was attempting to present a framework for global management that encompasses management theory and practice from around the world. Positing four domains of management, he explores how different cultures have predominant attractions to different domains. He's interested in how left-brain/right-brain research and the Oriental concept of Ying/Yang are both contributing to a growing tendency to integrate across domains. He notes the Japanese concept of mutual interest gradually appearing in Western leadership and organizational theory, traditionally dominated by self-interest.

Four Global Management Domains

- **Primal:** Focus on the basics; concern for the tangible and for people; generating pride, enthusiasm and love
- **Rational:** Focus on effective management of resources, converting capabilities into results
- **Developmental:** Products and markets evolve in stages; collaboration overtakes competition
- **Metaphysical:** Focus on the flow, velocity, quality and quantity of energy; drawing from both ancient wisdom and modern physics

Globality

According to Harold Sirkin, James Hemerling and Arindam Bhattachara, in the new global reality we will all eventually be competing or collaborating with everyone from everywhere for everything. The successful companies will be continually scanning the world for competitors, potential partners and new ideas. They will be doing business in ways that bring together the best practices and strategies developed over centuries in the Occidental and Oriental worlds. In their book *Globality*, they tell the remarkable stories of companies that achieved worldwide success, suggesting that we might soon be recognizing that:

- The fastest growing global brands are Goodbaby, Embraer, Tata, BYD, Cemex, Bharat Forge
- The most celebrated business leaders are Wang Chuanfu, Lorenzo Zambrano and Anand Mahindra
- Your daughter's first choice for an MBA just might be Skolkovo Business School outside Moscow
- Your next favourite car could be a snappy new Dongfeng

The Renaissance City

The phrase "think globally, act locally," originally associated with the environmental movement, is now widely applied to the challenge of effective action in the face of overwhelming complexity and interconnection. While nothing is now purely local – with every local action both influenced by and influencing broader global forces – local action is the antidote to the paralysis that could take hold from too intense contemplation of the full global picture.

The locus of economic and creative activity in the Italian Renaissance was the city-state – Florence initially, but by the early 16th century Venice and Rome. Today, as capital and ideas flow freely across national boundaries, the spotlight is once again being put on the role of cities in driving innovation and wealth-creation. It is in cities that we find the critical mass of diverse perspectives, knowledge, and skills that produces innovation: technological and social innovation, innovation in products and services, innovation in how work gets done and institutions are designed and managed.

We said earlier that at a country level, location now matters less. Some have posited that since the Internet, modern telecommunication and transportation systems have made it no longer necessary for people who work together to be together, "place" has no importance in the knowledge economy. Richard Florida counters this "geography is dead" myth by noting:

> Not only do people remain highly concentrated, but the economy itself – the high-tech, knowledge-based and creative-content industries that drive so much of economic growth – continues to concentrate in specific places from Austin and Silicon Valley to New York City and Hollywood, just as the automobile industry once concentrated in Detroit. Students of urban and regional growth from Robert Park and Jane Jacobs to Wilbur Thompson have long pointed to the role of places as incubators of creativity, innovation and new industries (Rise of the Creative Class, p.219).

The difference, according to Florida, is that the cradles of the new economy are not thriving for such traditional economic reasons as access to natural resources, transportation routes, tax breaks or business incentives, but rather because creative people want to live there. The companies then follow the people – or, in many cases, are started by them. Creative centers provide the integrated eco-system or habitat where all forms of creativity – artistic and cultural, technological and economic – can take root and flourish (p. 218).

Arguing in *The Rise of the Creative Class* that nearly half of all wage and salary income in the US is now generated by what he calls "the creative class" – scientists, engineers, artists, musicians, designers and knowledge-based professionals – Florida suggests that the key challenge for cities that aspire to be economic winners in the new economy is understanding what attracts creative people to a place. In our terms, they need to recognize the characteristics of a Renaissance City.

Florida explores the interrelated set of factors that work together to create a "quality of place," attractive to creative people:

- *What's there:* the combination of the built environment and the natural environment; a proper setting for pursuit of creative lives?

- *Who's there*: the diverse kinds of people, interacting and providing cues that anyone can plug into and make a life in that community?

- *What's going on:* the vibrancy of street life, café culture, arts, music and people engaging in outdoor activities – altogether a lot of active, exciting, creative endeavors?

One of the things that attracts talent to a city is multiple career opportunities in their field. As Florida notes in his reference to Hollywood and Silicon Valley, while the world is flat in the sense that interconnectivity has begun to level the playing field, it is also "lumpy." Centres of excellence stand out against the flat landscape – Mumbai for technology, London for financial services, Silicon Valley for high tech industry. These are places where clusters of like-minded firms have grouped together to build a powerful business community – competing and collaborating in turn, and spawning the creation of support services and infrastructure.

Local action for global change

Under "leading systemic change," we explore Margaret Wheatley's work on how new understandings in the scientific world can provide new insight into organizations. She further suggests that quantum perceptions of reality may help us understand why thinking globally and acting locally is exactly the right approach. Acting locally – working with the system you can get your arms around – has always been considered a sound strategy for changing large systems. Newtonian science would say that each local act creates incremental change, and "little by little, system by system, we develop enough momentum to affect the larger society."

But if you take the quantum view that space everywhere is filled with fields – "invisible, non-material structures that are the basic substance of the universe," then you might imagine that:

> These changes in small places, however, create large-systems change, not because they build one upon the other, but because they share in the unbroken wholeness that has united them all along. Our activities in one part of the whole create non-local causes that emerge far from us. There is value in working with the system any place it manifests because unseen connections will create effects at a distance, in places we never thought. This model of change - of small starts, surprises, unseen connections, quantum leaps - matches our experience more closely than our favored models of incremental change (pp. 42-43).

Chapter 6: Accelerating Cross Boundary Learning

We have seen, and will see elsewhere in this journey, how exposure to discoveries in one discipline opens up new lines of thinking and innovation in another – the application of scientific exploration of systems thinking and quantum physics to business and how we understand organizations, for example. Peter Drucker, in several of his writings, has pointed out that the changes that affect a body of knowledge most profoundly do not, as a rule come out of its own domain. For example, "After Gutenberg first used moveable type; there was practically no change in the craft of printing for 400 years – until the steam engine came in."

The Italian Renaissance saw breakthroughs in every aspect of human endeavour: in architecture and biology, painting and astronomy, cartography and medicine, literature and chemistry, sculpture and political economy. Perhaps this explosion of innovation was at least in part attributable to a sense that the rigid barriers had not yet gone up between the professional disciplines. Key players in one field were often players or influencers in another. Young people were not streamed into either art or science early in their education. Intuition and reason could be spoken of in the same breath. Renaissance Florence did not take the view that engineers were by definition illiterate, and artists incapable of running anything.

A Definition of Innovation:

> *A process for extracting economic and social value from knowledge. Putting ideas, knowledge and technologies to work in a manner that brings about a significant improvement in performance.*

It has become an axiom of the global knowledge economy that the ability to learn and innovate faster and better than the competition is now the key to sustaining competitive advantage and success. In this context, the notion of what learning means and how it's done well is being richly explored. Learning no longer conjures up the image of the youth apprenticed to a trade (or the tasks of household management) for six or seven years then applying the learning without much variation beyond gradual improvement in proficiency for the rest of his or her life. We've moved beyond the idea that learning means children in neat classroom rows being drilled in reading, writing, and 'rithmetic. We now talk of lifelong learning, learning organizations, action learning, and agile learning. As the Internet makes information on every imaginable topic widely available across the globe, we also worry about how to make sense of it all — make meaning, turn data into knowledge, then manage that knowledge.

Learning is work/work is learning

If the truly unique contribution of management in the 20th century was the 50-fold increase in the productivity of the manufacturing worker, according to Drucker the most important management challenge for the 21st century is how to increase the productivity of knowledge work and the knowledge worker. If knowledge work is fundamentally about the creation and application of ideas, then the implication is that learning is a new form of labour. Far from being something that requires time out from engaging in productive activity, it is at the heart of productive activity.

This concept is at the core of approaches like "action learning" codified by Kolb and others starting in the 1970s. The continued popularity of action learning approaches reflects the failure of conventional leadership development to translate into practical increases in organizational performance. While it is highly useful to take individuals out of their daily routine periodically to be exposed to new ideas and receive intense coaching, this in itself will not create effective leaders. Leaders return to their organizational context without necessarily having developed the skills to translate their individual learning to organizational learning, to apply it to practical problems, to use it proactively to drive innovation.

Action learning approaches tend to assume that the starting point of learning for most adults is experiencing/doing. They treat the workplace as the classroom and real-life problems as the learning vehicles. The Galileo Educational Network, for example, has been using action learning – something now generally referred to as authentic learning tasks – as a basis for inspiring children in classrooms across North America, with great success (see www.galileo.org).

Learning with the whole brain

A popular book published in the late 1970s was Betty Edwards' *Drawing on the Right Side of the Brain,* which claimed that anyone with sufficient ability to thread a needle or catch a baseball could learn to draw – not necessarily become a great master, but develop an acceptable competence. Far from being a magical ability possessed by only a few:

> *The magical mystery of drawing ability seems to be, in part at least, an ability to make a shift in brain state to a different mode of seeing/perceiving. When you see in the special way in which experienced artists see, then you can draw....My aim is to provide the means for releasing that potential, for gaining access at a conscious level to your inventive, intuitive, imaginative powers that may have been largely untapped by our verbal, technological culture and educational system...From this experience you will develop your ability to perceive things freshly in their totality, to see underlying patterns and possibilities for new combinations. Creative solutions to problems, whether personal or professional, will be accessible through new modes of thinking and new ways of using the power of your brain (pp. 3, 5-6).*

We have said that multi-disciplinary learning is important because innovation so often happens when ideas from divergent knowledge domains come together in novel ways. But multi-disciplinary learners are also much more likely to be exercising different parts of their brain, to be accessing their whole intelligence. Howard Gardner has posited the importance of becoming adept in applying a range of different "intelligences". He suggests seven, but we have reduced them here to six:

The Intelligences

1. **Verbal-linguistic intelligence**—involving a sensitivity to the meaning, order, sounds and rhythms of words and the functions and powers of language.

2. **Musical intelligence**—the ability to "hear" music in one's mind, to compose and to think musically, especially in terms of melody and rhythm.

3. **Logical-mathematical intelligence**—the ability to use reasoning, ordering and logical thought for problem solving, whether in mathematics and science or in the ordinary affairs of life.

4. **Visual-spatial intelligence**—including the ability to perceive accurately, to visualize and to create artistic transformations of the visual word.

5. **Bodily-kinesthetic intelligence**—as exemplified in people like dancers and athletes who develop unusual mastery over the motions of the body.

6. **The personal intelligences**—including two aspects: The ability to access one's own inner feelings and the ability to understand and be able to relate to other people.

Making Meaning

In the days when each manuscript was painstakingly written and illuminated by hand, access to information beyond one's small local sphere was a luxury available to very few. Today, as the

Internet has made the explosion of available information triggered by the printing press look puny by comparison, the learning challenge is not so much finding information as making meaning and creating knowledge.

There are a variety of ways to think about this challenge. At the most tactical level, organizations are thinking about knowledge management systems that provide ready access to the collective memory of the organization to all within it, in a practical, useable format. The best of such systems are technology enabled, driven by a very clear view of why the system is being created and how it will be used.

At a more strategic level, Renaissance Leaders are thinking about how to distill the essence of meaning from masses of information, and communicate it to others in a simple, impactful way. Systems thinking and the kind of recognition of frequently recurring patterns we discuss in that section play a role here. Given that the telling and hearing of stories has been central to how cultures define themselves and create community for as long as there has been language, it's not surprising that the language of literature often creeps into the dialogue about how to make meaning. Ikujiro Nonaka writes in an HBR article in the early 90's about how Japanese companies drew on metaphors and similes to focus the collective knowledge of teams around a product or service challenge: If the automobile were an organism, how would it evolve? If we thought of the drum of a copy machine as a beer can – which costs very little to manufacture – where would that lead us? Storytelling has emerged as an essential leadership capability in the drive to understand and apply cross-boundary learning.

Chapter 7: Thinking Back from the Future

In *Beyond Certainty: A Personal Odyssey*, Charles Handy recalls the liberating moment when he realized the one message he'd taken away from all his schooling was not only crippling but wrong. That message was that every major problem in life had already been solved, and the aim of education was to transfer the answers from the teacher to him. The realization that this was not true, he says, changed his life:

> The world is not an unsolved puzzle, waiting for the occasional genius to unlock its secrets. The world, or most of it, is an empty space waiting to be filled....I did not have to wait and watch for the puzzles to be solved; I could jump into the space myself. I was free to try out my ideas, invent my own scenarios, create my own futures. Life, work, and organization could become a self-fulfilling prophecy, with my making the prophecies... (p. 17).

Most definitions of leadership incorporate the notion that leaders create and articulate a compelling vision that inspires their followers: They see the long view, paint a concrete picture of a desired future, effectively communicate and manage the dream. For Renaissance Leaders, putting their lively imaginations to work on exploring possible futures and using what they find there to guide their actions in the present is both second nature and a finely honed skill. Renaissance Leaders can imagine and articulate what an organization needs to be 10-20 years "out" from the current reality and have a sense of direction and a pathway to get back from the future to now.

Notice that we don't say *have a plan to move from now to the future*, but a plan to *get back from the future to now*. It's a crucial difference. Given that the future isn't a straight line from the present, there is a need to fully understand the stages of development through which the organization will have to pass working backwards from the future. These stages may look very different from those that might be developed if you worked from now to the future.

Beyond the rear-view mirror

Historically, organizations have managed largely through a rear-view mirror, relying heavily on measures of past performance to plan the future. They have focused on "lag indicators" – looking back – as opposed to "lead indicators" – predictive measures of the future. Using lag indicators often implies that we know the way in which these shape the performance of an organization, a market or a system. But if the future is different from the present, lag indicators are often measures of an old way of working, not the new.

More and more, companies are investing in identifying and learning how to use predictive indictors – such as shifts in customer perception of the value a business offers versus its competitors, or leading economic indicators such as housing starts, retail price index or GDP growth. Only a few regularly supplement this past/present view of the world with a disciplined approach to exploring possible futures, looking for risks and opportunities.

Consider this proposition. Given how rapidly and constantly the global knowledge economy is changing, many of today's schoolchildren will find themselves working in jobs that don't yet exist, creating products that have not yet been imagined. A teacher looking at education through a rear-view mirror might complain that students today are hyperactive, have short attention spans, no discipline and no respect – worse, they actually treat teachers as their equals!

A teacher imagining a future in which core competencies include systems thinking, a lively curiosity, a global mindset, an ability to collaborate, multi-task and understand non-linear approaches might watch a student at a computer through a different lens. Perhaps these children are in fact developing strong foundational skills for future success as visualization specialists, web gardeners, tacit knowledge catchers, nanofabricators, robot trainers, windfinders, bioinformationalists – or Renaissance Leaders? Working back from the future provides a radically different perspective on the same behaviour than the one we see if we look just from the present.

Take another example. There is a growing shortage of fresh water in the world at the same time that the demand for water is increasing. Mexico, for example, is currently extracting a great deal of its freshwater from aquifers, reducing the potential of future supply. Saudi Arabia has water for another ten years or so and then faces real difficulty. If we imagine a future where all water has to be imported into a country and water usage has to be curtailed, we can quickly see how different a plan this would be from one in which we looked at current demand and supply levels and sought simply to increase water use efficiency. We can also envisage social unrest over water supply (Nairobi already had a water riot in July 2007), especially where access to water is based on wealth, not need. Smart money is moving to new technologies for desalination, water reuse and recycling, and water control.

Rehearsing the future

Conventional wisdom in the early 1970s held that the price of oil would stay stable. When it rose suddenly and dramatically in the mid-70s in the wake of what became known in the Western world as "the oil crisis," Royal Dutch/Shell was already prepared to drastically change its business in response. They had already "rehearsed" this future. Borrowing techniques employed in military planning in World War II, Pierre Wack and his colleagues had developed a tool for preparing the company to deal with a variety of possible futures, putting a strong focus on imagining futures that were not widely expected to happen. What became known as "scenario planning" rejects the idea of the future as a straight-line extrapolation of current trends, considering instead the broad range of forces shaping the local and global environments and the alternate futures they might drive.

Such scenario planning is again in use today, as most analysts predict oil will reach $200 a barrel by 2015, and stay at or above that price. The impact on all of our lives will be substantial. The impact on transport and food costs was already apparent when oil was at around $130/barrel. Renaissance Leaders are already imagining a future very different from the present – one in which alternative means of communication, new food sources, and new methods of food distribution are occurring. New retail forms and new global supply chains will also be created.

As a tool and a discipline, scenario planning exhibits the Renaissance tendency to cross discipline boundaries and integrate left- and right-brain thinking. While scenario planning may have been born in the military, it draws heavily on the world of literature. Peter Schwartz, examining the history and practice of scenario planning in *The Art of the Long View*, states:

> It is a common belief that serious information should appear in tables, graphs, numbers, or at least sober scholarly language. But important questions about the future are usually too complex or imprecise for the conventional languages of business and science. Instead we use the language of stories and myths. Stories have a psychological impact that graphs and equations lack. Stories are about meaning; they help explain <u>why</u> things happen in a certain way. They give order and meaning to events – a crucial aspect of understanding future

possibilities....They open people to multiple perspectives, because they allow them to describe how different characters see in events the meaning of those events. Moreover, stories help people cope with complexity (pp. 40-41).

Scenarios provide a way of having a conversation about the future – giving shape and meaning, and creating frameworks for a dialogue. More significantly, they can provide a basis for analyzing trends and information, and building models. A great deal of our understanding of climate change comes from just such work.

But scenario planning is only one tool of strategic foresight. There are others. Key amongst them is understanding potential discontinuity – the disruptive power of some new development, especially a new technology or new patterns of social behaviour.

When the Internet began to be widely available in 1993-94, few imagined it would radically change the way in which the world works. But it has. The music industry, financial services and the travel industry have all faced major changes in how they operate. In the case of the music industry, the Internet has led to the collapse of traditional ways of buying and selling music, as well as the creation of new supply chains and new patterns of consumer behaviour.

With wireless broadband technology becoming more powerful and widely available, and digital devices – not just computers, but Internet-enabled hand-held devices – capable of receiving information and data at very high speeds, we can expect more disruptions, most especially in education, health and financial services.

Creating the future

"...vision without systems thinking ends up painting lovely pictures of the future with no deep understanding of the forces that must be mastered to move from here to there."

Peter Senge, <u>The Fifth Discipline (p. 12)</u>

Critiques of scenario planning argue that too often it becomes an esoteric exercise that may create interesting stories, but rarely leads to productive change in organizations. Renaissance Leaders have developed the skill of connecting their imagined futures with deep learning from the past to guide their choices in the present. Systematically looking at the future while at the same time developing an understanding of history of a particular issue, idea, opportunity or region enables Renaissance Leaders to ground their thinking in time and space.

"Strategic foresight" has emerged as a useful discipline in this regard. Fusing "futures" methods such as scenario planning with strategic management, strategic foresight stresses that the point of visiting the future in your imagination is to use what you see to chart the most successful course toward it – to detect adverse conditions, guide policy, shape strategy, explore new markets/products/services.

Strategic Foresight: A Definition

This is a simple definition of strategic foresight, one commonly used by teachers of the discipline:

> *"the general ability to create and maintain a high quality, coherent and functional forward view, and to use insights arising in useful organizational ways"*

This definition leads practitioners to undertake three different kinds of foresight work:

> **Pragmatic foresight** – aimed at carrying out tomorrow's business better by seeking to be systematic about understanding the future
>
> **Progressive foresight** – going beyond conventional thinking and practices and reformulating processes, products and services using quite different assumptions so as to position the organization as ahead of the competition or first to act in the light of changing conditions
>
> **Civilizational foresight** – that seeks to understand the aspects of the next civilization to which a community or region is moving – for example, Zimbabwe twenty years from now.

The primary methods of strategic foresight are:

• **Scenario Planning and Review** - using a variety of methods for exploring the factors that may shape the scenario

• **Trend Analysis, modified for certain risks** - a form of scenario planning using hard data to look at "what if?"

• **Uncertainty Analysis** - that looks at the disruptive and likely events that will change how an activity is being undertaken. These can be statistical models, historically based observations or speculative. This is also known as "What If Analysis"

• **Risk Analysis** - that uses the rigorous processes now associated with risk analysis to look at the likely outcomes of a process

• **Delphi Process** - that uses experts (potentially in large numbers) in a rigorous process for soliciting responses to key ideas and placing them in order of importance

- **Challenge Dialogue System™** - a systematic, template-driven process for engaging a community of interest (e.g. a cross section of leaders associated with the fibre industry sector worldwide)

- **Back-Casting / Historical Analysis** - Looking from the future back. For example, offering the Annual Report of the Alberta Chamber of Resources for 2025 and seeing what issues this raises

- **Transformative Cycle** - developed by Richard Slaughter and others in Australia, this uses a set of models of change to identify the patterns of change within an industry (the industry S curve) and then looks at where a particular technology is in relation to that cycle (the T-cycle). For example, Ray Kurzweil provides an analysis of the speed at which information processing technologies are replaced, which in turn provides a basis for understanding the future of the data industry and the needed development and investment patterns

- **Causal Layered Analysis** - developed by Sohail Inayatullah (a leading futurist and coeditor of the *Journal of Future Studies*), this method uses a variety of different approaches (layers of understanding) to understand in depth the drivers for different future scenarios. UNESCO has used this method to look at educational systems and literacy. Some countries have used it to look at the future of health systems

All of these methods rely on: (a) an ability to access thought-leaders in the chosen area of work and to explore with them their understanding of the current situation (a test of their reality) as well as their understanding of what is likely to happen over the next 20-40 years; (b) an ability to access the most reliable, current and verifiable data about the performance and trends within a sector – e.g. biotechnology; (c) the ability to work in a workshop mode to develop scenarios that may involve individuals "suspending" current beliefs so as to fully understand the implications of a scenario; and (d) the ability to test ideas and "tentative conclusions" with industry leaders and others, whether or not they were involved in the generation of the framework.

The point of being rigorous about foresight – being strategic – is that it can provide a basis for rethinking the way we do business and repositioning an organization to take advantage of the future before others do so. It's about shaping the Renaissance.

Chapter 8: Leading Systematic Change

In the global knowledge economy, the pace of change is accelerating exponentially and the challenges are becoming increasingly complex – think climate change, international terrorism, global food security and pandemics. The odds are that a Renaissance Leader will be regularly engaged in leading change – and that more often than in any other period in history, this will mean helping organizations make fundamental changes to what they do and how they operate.

The problem, as David Nadler has pointed out, is that today's organizations have been designed specifically for stability, to provide a buffer from changes in the outside world. Noting how Bismarck's small World War I German army – that had learned much from Max Weber's invention in the late 19th century of "bureaucracy," with its attendant standard procedures, rules, roles, and lines of communication – managed to outmaneuver the "sprawling feudal Russian army," he argues that asking 20th century organizations to change is:

> ...kind of like taking draft horses that were bred, one generation after another, to pull heavy loads and then demanding to know why they can't win the Kentucky Derby. The organizational design most of us have grown up with is just as much a product of natural selection – and it was bred to resist change (p. 307).

Exacerbating the problem is the fact that the Industrial Era mentality encourages taking things apart to find the one piece that needs to be fixed. Organizations looking for a saviour in the latest change fad – be it process re-engineering or team-building in the wilderness – will inevitably be disappointed, because they tend to focus on fragmented, one-off actions. They ignore the "web of relationships that make up the organization."

Organizations as congruent systems

In the mid-1970s, Nadler, then a professor at Columbia University, became intrigued by work being done in the physical sciences on systems. It's a simple enough concept: a system as a set of elements that takes input from the environment, subjects it to some form of transformation, produces an output – and, the most interesting facet – has the capacity to alter both input and transformation processes based on how output was received or responded to, in other words using feedback to change.

Nadler, his colleague Michael Tushman, and others at Stanford and MIT following parallel tracks began examining businesses through the lens of systems thinking. The result, for Nadler, was the creation of the "congruence model," that has been the foundation of a successful career helping CEOs lead change. The congruence model describes an organization as a system that takes input (in the form of everything that's happening in its environment, the resources both human and material available to it, and the past events and crises that have shaped it), then makes a set of decisions on how to configure resources vis-à-vis the demands, opportunities and constraints of the environment within the context of history. This determines the type of transformation process to which the input will be subjected, in order to produce outputs at the system, unit and individual level – products, services, earnings, and employment.

Nadler replaces the traditional picture of the organization as a hierarchical chart of roles and reporting relationships with a systems view that shows the interaction among:

The "hardware" of the organization- the work to be done and the formal organization of structures, systems, processes grouping people and work and coordinating their activities; and

Its "software"- the skills and dreams and attitudes of the people doing the work, and the informal organization – the culture, values, beliefs, patterns of communication and influences – how things really get done.

It's called the congruence model, because what matters is "fit" amongst the components. Change one aspect in any of these boxes, and the whole system is out of whack. That's why the concept of integrated change, change that is constantly thinking about the interplay of every aspect of the organization, is so important.

> *Suppose for the moment that you could build your own dream car. You might take the styling of a Jaguar, the power plant of a Porsche, the suspension of a BMW, and the interior of a Rolls-Royce. Put them together and what have you got? Nothing. Why? Because they weren't designed to go together. They don't fit.*

- *Noted systems theorist Russell Ackoff, quoted in Nadler, (p. 27).*

While the model looks very static and left-brain in two dimensions, in application it's highly dynamic. Says Nadler:

> *...it's important to view the congruence model as a tool for organizing your thinking about any organizational situation, rather than as a rigid template you can use to dissect, classify and compartmentalize what you observe. It's a way to make sense out of a constantly changing kaleidoscope of information and impressions – a way to think about organizations as movies rather than snapshots....Your challenge is to digest and interpret the constant flow of pictures – the relationships, the interactions, the feedback loops – all the elements that make an organization a living organism (p. 43).*

Systems thinking as the "fifth discipline"

Peter Senge was a student at MIT at the time Nadler and others were first beginning to think this way, and was fascinated to find business leaders visiting the science department there to learn about systems thinking. Over the years, he has come to regard systems thinking as an important antidote to the "sense of helplessness that many feel as we enter 'the age of interdependence'," overwhelmed by complexity and more information than we can possibly absorb:

> Systems thinking is a discipline for seeing wholes. It is a framework for seeing interrelationships rather than things, for seeing patterns of change rather than static "snapshots"….It is also a set of specific tools and techniques, originating in two threads: in "feedback" concepts of cybernetics and in "servo-mechanism" engineering theory dating back to the nineteenth century. During the last thirty years, these tools have been applied to understand a wide range of corporate, urban, regional, economic, political, ecological, and even physiological systems" (p. 68).

Senge's personal contribution in this arena has been helping leaders shift their mindset "from seeing ourselves as separate from the world to connected to the world, from seeing problems as caused by someone or something 'out there' to seeing how our own actions create the problems we experience (pp. 12-13)." He helps leaders recognize the simple, archetypal patterns that underlie complex situations (all the more difficult to do because we are part of the pattern) determine what systemic change has the highest leverage, and lead that change in the organization.

Lessons from the new sciences

Margaret Wheatley suggests we are only in the very early stages of understanding what science can teach us about systems thinking and how it applies to organizations and leadership. If the 20th century organization was designed using assumptions from 17th century Newtonian images of the universe – largely machine-based and focused on dissecting the parts – what can the 21st century organization learn from the new sciences of quantum physics, self-organizing systems and chaos theory?

In the early 1990s, Wheatley set out on a journey to explore such questions as: "Why do so many organizations feel dead? Why do projects take so long, develop ever-greater complexity, yet so often fail to achieve any truly significant results? Why does progress, when it appears, so often come from unexpected places, or as a result of surprises or serendipitous events that our planning had not considered? (p. 1)" Immersing herself in the "new sciences," she discovered a new world:

> ...where order and change, autonomy and control were not the great opposites that we had thought them to be. It was a world where change and constant creation signaled new ways of maintaining order and structure. I was reading of chaos that contained order; of information as the primal, creative force; of systems that, by design, fell apart so they could renew themselves; and of invisible forces that structured space and held complex things together (pp. 1-2).

In 1992's *Leadership and the New Sciences*, she felt she was just beginning to apply these understandings to her work helping organizations change and be effective – looking for patterns of movement over time rather than analyzing parts to death, focusing on structures that might facilitate relationships rather than detailed planning and analysis.

Collaboration as the DNA of high-performing organizations

Systems are fundamentally about relationships. Systemic change involves constantly getting all interdependent and moving parts into a proper relationship with the environment and each other to foster organizational health. It's no wonder, then, that organizations are increasingly interested in collaboration – which the Innovation Expedition considers the very DNA of the high-performing organization in the knowledge economy. With information technology making it possible to keep geographically dispersed people connected and productive, the role of networks as the soft infrastructure bringing together the expertise to solve complex problems and lead systemic change is coming to the fore.

Chapter 9: Drive Performance with a Passion

We have characterized Renaissance Leadership as a particular way of looking at and understanding the world, as a mindset, a way of thinking/doing/being. Renaissance Leadership is equally about delivering results. Renaissance Leaders care deeply about making the world a better place and have a passionate focus on performance at all levels – individual, team, organization. Their goals are as diverse as their interests. They seek to create profitable organizations that are also socially responsible and sought-after by employees as wonderful places to work. They strive to build sustainable prosperity in communities: jobs, wealth creation, people-oriented social services, a vibrant arts and culture sector, quality of life. They are committed to halting environmental degradation and climate change. They want to do away with poverty and injustice, and eliminate global inequity.

Setting the tone

Renaissance Leaders set the tone for organizational performance by talking about their personal goals in concrete terms – terms that reflect the desired outcomes, not just a checklist of activities. They share with their teams the high expectations they have of themselves and how these connect to the larger organizational purpose. They describe how they do regular check-ins with themselves or a coach on whether they're performing at a level that reflects their full capability. They are concrete and clear about the collective results the team is driving toward, and how they're going to get there. We suggest that in a high-performing organization in the global knowledge economy, there is much talk about:

- **Innovation:** The fact that in times of fundamental change, it is the innovators who survive and thrive. That innovation occurs at the individual, organizational, and inter-organizational levels, and can take the form of technological or social change. It can involve a product, a process, a business model, an organizational structure, a strategy or a system. Innovation is a discipline that can be learned

- **Collaboration:** That innovation usually results from collaborative efforts – collaboration within the organization, but especially with outside parties such as suppliers, customers, competitors. That networks provide a collaborative structure to bring together all the expertise required to turn a good idea into reality quickly and efficiently – without the cost in both money and time of creating a complex formal structure, and without constraints of geography

- **Learning:** That the ability to gather, create and integrate new knowledge quickly is a source of competitive advantage. That getting better at learning from experience and sharing knowledge across the organization is critical. That learning is more than keeping up with developments in one's specialized field. It's about an intense and wide-ranging curiosity, an openness to ideas that seem incredible, a desire to seek and use feedback

- **Integrity:** That great performance is driven by a compelling purpose. That the organization has a set of values that inform every decision, every action, and every conversation. It is clear on its social responsibility and how it will live up to it

- **Focus:** That activity for the sake of activity is just wasting energy. That before launching into a task, every individual must understand how that task connects to the larger purpose and strategy of the organization, and why this task takes priority over other possible uses of valuable time

- **Humour:** That fun and laughter are not only allowed but essential. That in a world of uncertainty, the keys to success include flexibility, spontaneity, unconventionality, shrewdness, playfulness, and humility.

Mapping the destination

We believe that improving the productivity of knowledge workers is the central task of Renaissance Leaders in a global, knowledge economy. A chronic challenge is measuring the return on investments made in people and associated costs, physical infrastructure, technology – especially when the output is a knowledge product or a service rather than a tangible thing. It's rarely easy to make a direct link between a single output and a broader outcome, which is impacted by multiple variables. As a fall-back position, organizations tend to focus on measuring the amount of activity generated: numbers of meetings, reports, workshops. This makes it very easy for people to become consumed in unproductive "busy work."

Outcome maps and logic models are useful tools for getting leadership teams aligned on the business case for proposed work, for giving employees or team members a holistic view of what they're working toward, and for creating a performance measurement framework. An outcome map identifies business outcomes that align with and support an organization's strategic objectives, as well as the actions required to achieve them. It serves as a "roadmap" for turning strategy into action, and a framework for building a clear logic model and a customized balanced scorecard for tracking performance.

A logic model captures as simply as possible on one page the complex story of:

- Why you're doing what you're doing (challenges, issues, drivers, opportunities)

- What you're investing (resources)

- What you're actually doing (activities)

- What's produced as a result (outputs)

- What changes as a result (outcomes)

Renaissance Leaders develop the ability to use outcome maps and logic models as the "inner voice" of their journey to high performance. They can articulate the logic of their journey at any time – it is their map. Some have such models on display, some use them as a basis for dialogue with their colleagues, and others simply understand this logic.

Measuring progress

The logic model describes the destination; now you need a way of measuring progress towards it. In developing the concept of a balanced scorecard, R. Kaplan and D. Norton of the Harvard Business School were underscoring the point that it is not sufficient to track the traditional financial metrics. Measures of revenue and earnings are backward-looking, capturing the company's success in the last quarter or year, and not necessarily predictive of future success. While share price in theory includes a forward-looking element (investors bet on the company's future success), dramatic swings in the market highlight just how tenuous this link can be in reality.

Through the 90s, large corporations were reminded of what proprietors of local "mom-and-pop shops" know all too well— that customer satisfaction, loyalty, and perception of value are the key to sustained revenue and profit growth. They began to recognize and measure how employee engagement/commitment and internal business processes

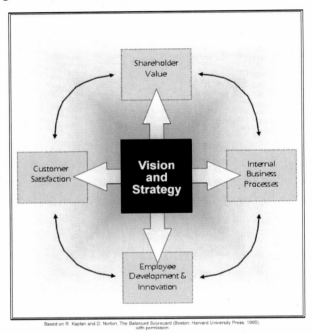

Based on R. Kaplan and D. Norton, The Balanced Scorecard (Boston, Harvard University Press, 1995), with permission

contributed to customer satisfaction and shareholder value. The concept of a balanced scorecard took hold.

While the classic balanced scorecard model is a useful beginning, its power is in starting a conversation within an organization as to what measures will be meaningful in its specific context. This is true in companies, not-for-profits, or public sector organizations. In a not-for-profit, for example, "shareholder value" prompts a discussion of appropriate measures of funder/donor satisfaction or intent to continue to contribute. In many organizations, new categories of measures such as community impact or corporate social responsibility quickly emerge.

For each category on their scorecard, we urge organizations to choose no more than one or two key metrics for the purposes of broad-based communication within the organization and to external stakeholders. While in many organizations there will be a need to track much more detailed management information to keep on course, the purpose of the balanced scorecard is to give a snapshot view of organizational health and ability to sustain performance. If it becomes overly complicated, it's less useful as a tool to engage stakeholders in conversations around organizational performance.

It is also possible for individuals in the organization to have their own balanced scorecards – the measures they need to achieve for their team to be successful. In one organization in which we worked, taking measurement down to the level of the person helped to transform mediocre performance into industry leadership in eight months.

The journey to high performance

Renaissance Leaders understand what it takes to achieve high performance. Our journey to date has focused on six core elements of their psyche that shape how they view and act in the world. But these six only begin to describe the challenges facing leaders of high-performing organizations. In our experience, such leaders:

- Have a vision and set of values that shape their work

- Have a clear strategy which does not change significantly over long periods of time – it is about the "rules" of the game and how the organization wishes to differentiate itself in the market

- Adapt quickly to changing market conditions and opportunities without losing their core values and integrity

- Recruit excellent people, invest in their development (building intellectual capital), and use appropriate methods to capture their knowledge

- Are rigorous about their internal processes and how their structure works

- Focus on speed, efficiency, and effectiveness

- Are outstanding in the way they work with their customers to build commitment and loyalty

- Understand the links among employee engagement $\Rightarrow$ customer loyalty $\Rightarrow$ profitability $\Rightarrow$ shareholder value, and manage these linkages effectively

- Are recognized as developing a best place to work and a best place with which to do business in the industry in which they operate

- Set themselves challenging goals which they frequently achieve – stretching the organization beyond what many think it is capable of

- Make mistakes because they take risks so as to be outstanding, and learn from these mistakes

- Engage and empower their people because they know the organization is focused and aligned around what has to be done

- Embrace constant change as a key to the fabric of the organization, and pursue change with the same rigour they would use for the management of any project

- Embrace technology as a vehicle for improving the performance of the people and systems in which they have invested

- Measure the right things often, but don't let measurement get in the way of performance

- Understand that profitability follows the effective use of all forms of organizational capital – intellectual capital, structural capital and customer capital – not the other way round. By allowing profits to flow, they focus and align the organization on what matters most

- Make decisions in real time and use time wisely to build the competency to make decisions at the right level throughout the organization

- Are effective and powerful communicators both inside the organization and with their customers and stakeholders

- Manage their supply chain (inbound and outbound logistics) effectively and partner with those in that chain to help improve their performance

- Create powerful and effective communities of customers and communicate with them with integrity, imagination and directness – developing customer loyalty

- Are perceptive and innovative, exhibiting grace under pressure, and departing from convention to achieve their vision without compromising the core values of the organization or their own integrity as leaders.

Each of these is a significant challenge requiring strong, focused leadership. Renaissance Leaders have confidence in their ability to take on such challenges, but are also modest about their role in the organization and able to laugh at their own performance. They take their challenge seriously and themselves less so.

Chapter 10:   Renaissance Leadership and Other Leadership Frameworks

Introduction

We have now described the context and practice of renaissance leadership, using these ideas as a way to focus our attention on the skills to lead organizations seeking high performance and sustainability in a global knowledge economy that is constantly changing.

Indeed, as we were developing these ideas and writing this book, established companies disappeared (Woolworth in Britain, Lehman Brothers in the US), the US government is now the majority shareholder in both GM and Chrysler and many other organizations have been transformed. New companies and new ways of doing business, both locally and globally, are emerging. "We live," according to the proverb, "in interesting times".

Renaissance leaders track developments and constantly use strategic foresight and their own understanding of patterns and systems to imagine a different future for their own organizations. They also engage others in the task of exploring this future and its day to day implications for "now". While we can all be surprised (and we are likely to be surprised many times in the future), the renaissance leader is constantly seeking to understand change as both a challenge and an opportunity – they are seeking meaning in the changes they see around them. They seek to communicate this meaning to their colleagues in a way that enables action.

But how does our understanding of renaissance leadership, outlined in this book, compare with other models of leadership? What is distinctive about renaissance leadership?

We asked several experienced executives, all of whom were studying at Athabasca University's Executive MBA program, to explore these questions with us. Their work was insightful and imaginative, as you will shortly see. Here we use their words to examine how renaissance leadership compares and contrasts with other theories of leadership. We first offer their review, and then we offer comments. In all, these executives looked at fifteen different leadership frameworks. Here, we use their work to look at five:

> Level Five Leadership
>
> Strategic Leadership
>
> Transformational Leadership
>
> Transactional Model
>
> Bureaucratic Leadership

What follows, in abbreviated form, are the observations made by our executives when they compared Renaissance Leadership with other contemporary leadership frameworks.

Level Five Leadership Framework[2]

Level Five Leadership is the description of leaders provided by Jim Collins in his book *Good to Great - Why Some Companies Make the Leap and Others Do Not* (2001). Such a leader "builds enduring greatness through a paradoxical blend of personal humility and professional will." These leaders are described as being timid and ferocious, shy and fearless and modest with a fierce, unwavering commitment to high standards.

Level Five Leadership and Renaissance Leadership have several vital similarities which make them both appropriate for leading through the 21st century and the current changes, opportunities and challenges in the business world and society. Level Five Leadership and Renaissance Leadership also employ

---

[2] We would like to especially thank Carly Clark for this contribution.

fundamental differences particularly regarding strategic development and preparation for the future, making them both unique.

From a broad perspective, the goals of both Renaissance Leadership and Level Five Leadership are improving and sustaining performance in a fast changing world. In both styles there is an emphasis on sustained value creation, developing a commitment from people, and planning for the future—all characteristics of 21st century and renaissance organizations. From the top down both Renaissance Leadership and Level Five Leadership are very similar in that the leaders recognize their strengths and weaknesses (Renaissance Leadership), or are aware of their limitations in a complex environment (Level Five Leadership). However, there are also some differences between the top level leaders and these styles. For example, level five leaders exhibit extreme humility and never take credit for their organization's success—their ambition is first and foremost their institution; whereas renaissance leaders don't appear to exhibit the same levels of modesty, although they are self-aware and do carry themselves with high integrity.

From an employee or subordinate standpoint, there are also several similarities. Level Five Leadership is entirely focused on people and ensuring the right people are in place before any thinking towards strategy is conceived. Also, Level Five Leadership is driven much more by character than competence; character is a must have in a Level Five Leadership environment whereas competence is viewed more as a bonus. Renaissance Leadership also has a strong focus for subordinates, but this mostly revolves around inspiring others and themselves for future performance. Although Level Five Leadership exhibits a clear focus on a disciplined culture, both leadership styles emphasize strong values, vision and passion as they strive towards better performance.

Renaissance Leadership places a strong emphasis on developing a capacity to innovate and looking for trends (in technology, organizational performance and sustainability) that will impact the future of the organization. This is a slightly different approach than Level Five Leadership. Level Five Leadership does encourage exploration of technology and breakthrough opportunities but a very cautious approach is taken for implementation by only integrating applications that fit very simply with the strengths, values and competencies of an organization.

In preparation for the future, Renaissance Leadership and Level Five Leadership take fairly different stances. Renaissance Leaders have a detailed plan and focus for dealing with and planning for the future. Through scenario planning, Renaissance Leadership attempts to develop a change strategy and is consistently planning and identifying a pathway to high performance in anticipation of the future. Although Level Five Leadership always has the future in mind and is striving to achieve long-term goals, the main indicated focus on working towards the future comes from the level five leaders ensuring that their successor is well beyond qualified to take over and continue to lead the company in the right direction.

The only other difference that stands out between Renaissance Leadership and Level Five Leadership is RL's emphasis on items outside the organization. For example, Renaissance Leadership has a heavy concentration on cross-boundary learning and connecting with other disciplines external to the organization, while Level Five Leadership does explore passion of the people and how the economics work best, external information seems to primarily be used for strategic decisions instead of simply increasing knowledge within an organization.

Strategic Leadership[3]

Strategic leadership "seeks to enhance performance while competing in turbulent and unpredictable environments", according to the authors Ireland & Hitt, in a paper they developed for the Academy of Management journal[4]). Strategic leadership allows a firm to be competitive and to achieve above average business results. "Strategic leadership is defined as a person's ability to anticipate, envision, maintain flexibility, think strategically, and work with others to initiate changes that will create a viable future for the organization"[5] . Strategic leadership also entails the possibility of achieving sustainable competitive advantage. This type of leadership is also sustainable within a global economy that is consistent with a very new competitive landscape, of uncertainty, changing and discontinuity.

The six key characteristics of renaissance leadership can be compared and contrasted to characteristics identified in the strategic model of leadership: determining the firm's purpose or vision, exploiting and maintaining core competencies, developing human capital, sustaining an effective organizational culture, emphasizing ethical practices, and establishing balanced organizational controls.

Renaissance Leadership	Strategic Leadership
Practice personal mastery-innovation is important and by demonstrating this importance others will be	**Emphasizing ethical practices-**leadership decisions based on honesty trust and

[3] We would like to thank Danielle Spence for her contribution to this section.
[4] Ireland, D. & Hitt, M. (2005). Achieving and maintaining strategic competitiveness in the 21st century: The role of strategic leadership: Academy of Management Executive, volume 19, No. 4.

[5] Ibid at page 6

inspired. Recognizing your own strengths and weaknesses as a leader.	integrity, this will inspire employees.
Apply a glocal mindset- understanding of the changes taking place on a global scale and being able to apply this to your own organization.	**Sustaining an effective organizational culture-** maintaining a learning environment, leading organizations that create and nurture knowledge.
Accelerate cross boundary learning- driving learning through every facet so that innovation will emerge and organizational performance will be improved.	**Exploiting and maintaining core competencies-**leaders working to apply these competencies so that organizational performance can be improved. These competencies can be resources and capabilities that cannot be imitated easily or may be too costly to implement by the competition (innovation).
Think back from the future- the leader envisioning of where they want to be in the future, and using this as the road map to guide current strategies.	**Determining the firm's purpose or vision-**it is important for a firm's leader with the help of its employees to develop a vision so that the organization is clear as to where the firm would like to go.

Lead systemic change-a leader who manages change through collaboration and teamwork across systems within organizations, communities, etc.	**Developing human capital**-leaders who view organizational citizenship as an important resource to develop, working on increasing the knowledge workforce.
Drive performance with a passion-leaders portray a high commitment to performance and a strong drive to achieve results.	**Establishing balanced organizational controls**-leaders maintain these controls (procedures that influence and guide work) so that performance goals can be achieved.

Renaissance leadership and strategic leadership are both about having the drive to increase the speed in which decisions are made; it is not only a top down approach it's about involving others. Its focus is on analyzing information from the outside for an organization to better itself from the inside. They are very similar because they both consider that knowledge work and workers are one of the primary drivers for economic growth.

Both models are consistent with a changing global environment. Sustainability in the 21st century is recognized by both models as important, renaissance leaders and strategic leaders agree that sustainability is necessary in order to stay competitive. Both models consider the effects of technological change and the rapidness that it is occurring at. They both focus on establishing and developing communities of practice from within the organization to leverage knowledge. However, strategic leadership also focuses on developing communities of practice with the outside as well, which the renaissance leadership fails to mention. The strategic leadership model definitely takes more of a stakeholder approach to leadership than renaissance leadership.

The challenges that face renaissance organizations and strategic leadership organizations differed slightly. For instance, renaissance organizations believed one of their major challenges in the 21st century was balancing the relationship between the different forms of capital such as intellectual, structural, customer, agility and collaborative capital. However strategic leadership organizations believe the major challenges in the 21st century are the global economy and the new competitive landscape.

Although both models are very similar, the renaissance leadership model looks from within more so then the strategic leadership model. Renaissance leadership is an inside out approach to leadership where as the strategic leadership model is more of an outside in approach to leadership. Renaissance leadership is very focused on its human capital from within where as strategic leadership focuses on the need for organizations to adapt to the significant changes in the global economy-the outside. "Strategic leaders will be challenged in the 21st century to mobilize citizens in ways that increase their adaptive abilities", say Ireland & Hitt.

Transformational Leadership and the Renaissance Leader[6]

Transformational Leadership is a leadership approach that is defined as leadership that creates valuable and positive change in followers. A transformational leader focuses on "transforming" others to help each other, to look out for each other, to be encouraging and harmonious, and to look out for the organization as a whole. In this leadership, the leader enhances the motivation, morale and performance of his follower group. Originally developed by J M Burns in a 1978

---

[6] We are grateful to Desa Hobbs for this contribution.

book simply called *Leadership* and then extended by the work of Bernard Bass in his 1985 book *Leadership and Performance*, this idea of leadership has a wide following.

Transformational Leadership focuses on similar themes to those developed in this account of the renaissance leader. These leaders are collaborative and are connected to their followers, supporting and encouraging them through a transformative process. Such transformative leadership incorporates both charismatic and visionary leadership that compels followers to achieve more than they usually would. For these reasons and the fact that transformational leadership involves emotions, ethics, and exceptional forms of influence, it is commonly an accepted and practiced style in many kinds of organizations.

There are a number of key and deliberate behaviors that are used by transformational leaders:

- *Idealized influence or Charisma* - These leaders are able to communicate their vision to followers, and as a result of the passion they convey in the belief of their own vision, compel others to follow and subscribe to their vision. Followers hold these leaders in high regard and are loyal to them.

- *Inspirational motivation* - Leaders who are skilled at encouraging and including staff involvement through the ability to inspire followers.

- *Individualized Consideration* - These leaders develop leadership potential in those that they lead by providing individualized mentorship to develop knowledge and confidence in followers.

- *Intellectual stimulation* - Transformational leaders include their constituents in problem solving and implementation of solutions. These leaders challenge the status quo and encourage innovation in their teams.

As can be seen in the comparative table below, there are similar themes that weave through both Transformational Leadership and Renaissance Leadership. Both of these frameworks for understanding leadership are directed at being supportive, collaborative and inspirational, to name a few qualities. It would be reasonable to surmise that the transformational leadership style was the precursor or catalyst for the birth or re-birth of renaissance leadership.

Renaissance Leadership	Transformational Leadership	Common themes across both leadership frameworks	Learning and knowledge development concepts
	Idealized influence or charisma	Both qualities of the **Transformational** leader highlight the ability to inspire and motivate followers. These qualities are closely related. Leaders display integrity and a charismatic personality. Common themes are seen in the **Renaissance** leaders practice personal mastery characteristic	These leaders participate in communities of practice and encourage the creation of learning organizations. They push themselves to do better and mentor and motivate followers to their personal best. These leaders recognize and reward leadership potential.
Practice personal mastery	Inspirational Motivation		
	Individualized consideration	**Transformational** leaders coach and develop followers. They focus on individualized needs of followers	These leaders create organizations of learning and implement systems thinking in their approach to problem solving
Lead systemic change		**Renaissance** leaders are able to bring teams together. They are change agents and are keenly aware of individual constituent needs to achieve a collective goal. **Renaissance** leaders have high expectations for themselves and others. To achieve goals and objectives these leaders engage others and inspire them to enlist in their cause. They are strong communicators, contributing to their inspiration, charisma and persuasiveness	
Drive performance with a passion			

Apply a glocal mindset	Intellectual stimulation	**Transformational** leadership encourages divergent thinking and development of innovative solutions.	These leaders are able to create and facilitate communities of learning and practice that create innovative solutions and ideas.
Accelerate cross-boundary learning		The **Renaissance** leader will investigate opportunities for learning outside of traditional sources seeking innovative opportunities globally and locally	
Think back from the future		**Renaissance** leaders are imaginative and encourage forward thinking	They apply strategic foresight skills.

Transactional Leadership[7]

Transactional leadership is a model that is still prevalent today. It is based on a reciprocal exchange between leaders and followers using reward and punishment to gain compliance from employees. The assumption with this type of leadership framework is that people are motivated by reward and punishment and that social systems work best with chain of command."

The following table is a comparison of the Transactional and Renaissance leadership models, in doing so providing a summary of the transactional approach.

---

[7] We are grateful to Harry Mah for this contribution.

Renaissance Leadership Characteristic	Transactional leadership Focus	Renaissance leadership focus
Personal Mastery	Western Philosophy, focus on technical tasks, managerial and control, personal mastery is not a focus	Eastern Philosophy, focus on self-awareness, inspiration, and leadership, development of personal mastery
Think back from the future	Reactive, think about the present	Visionary, think about the future, present, and past
Apply a glocal mindset	Focus on environment and department, local mindset	Focus on holistic and interest in changes around the world and how it impacts the organization, glocal mindset
Lead systemic change	Competitive, focus on task at hand, non systemic	Collaborative, interest in finding inter-connections, systemic thinking
Drive Performance with Passion	Distant, logical, focus on getting the task done	Feelings accepted and recognized, passion
Accelerate cross-	Focus on hierarchy,	Focus on networking and

boundary learning	linear learning, learning what is required for the job	cross boundary learning, creative, interest in many topics

The two approaches are clearly very different and distinctive, with transactional leadership being much more concerned with short to medium term results and renaissance leadership more focused on building a culture of performance linked to a strong innovative and responsive organization.

Bureaucratic Leadership[8]

Bureaucratic Leadership is a style of leadership that emphasizes procedures and historical methods regardless of their usefulness in changing environments. Bureaucratic leaders attempt to solve problems by adding layers of control, and their power comes from controlling the flow of information. Bureaucratic leaders ensure that policies and procedures are followed exactly and all activities are "by the book". While this form of leadership may be applicable to mitigate safety risks in certain industries, it is not appropriate in other areas because the inflexibility and high levels of control exerted can demoralize staff, and can diminish the organization's ability to react to changing external circumstances.

The bureaucratic leadership style is characterized by strict adherence to chain-of-command reporting and following rules precisely. These leaders impose strict and systematic discipline and are empowered via the office they hold, thereby using their bestowed authority and position power to lead. This type of leader is inclined to be very structured and follows the procedures as they have been established, often regardless of extenuating circumstances. There is no allowance for new problem-solving techniques and the established protocol can be

---

[8] We are grateful to Carolyn Dryden for this contribution.

very slow in effecting change due to the strict adherence to the organization's hierarchy. Bureaucratic leaders resist change or merely cope with forced change in order to return to the safe and routine processes of the organization. They do not embrace change nor do they reward creativity or innovative ideas.

In the following chart[9], the practices of renaissance leadership is described and contrasted with the practices of bureaucratic leadership. They are remarkably different.

[9] Adapted from a variety of sources, including Legacee, (2009). Bureaucracies impact on bureaucratic leadership. Retrieved April 25, 2009, from Legacee Web site: http://www.legacee.com/Info/Leadership/Bureaucratic.html

The Renaissance Leader will..	The Bureaucratic Leader will..
• Accept themselves and have a positive self-concept. • Not be afraid of making mistakes and will be receptive to criticism. • Have well-developed questioning and listening skills. • Have a generally positive regard for others and a tendency to trust them. • Be intensely interested in what they do and have a high level of energy. • Make work important and enjoyable while maintaining high standards for performance. • Clearly state the goals and vision for change. • Solicit input from throughout the organization. • Adapt internal changes to evolving external forces. • Anticipate new challenges.	• Always follow a set structure in the manner that it has been established. • Not explore new ways of problem solving. • Ensure that leadership has been defined in ways that fit the need for the organization to survive without risk. • Minimize creativity, personality, variation and emotion. • Maintain functional departments with clear distinctions in roles, responsibilities and reporting structures. • Adhere to short term and quantitative performance targets. • Monitor performance closely through formalized processes. • Offer financial rewards or promotions based on competency and administer penalties for failure. • Maintain vertical delegation, communication and

• Be a status quo challenger, a change creator and an innovation enthusiast. • Use empowerment and involvement strategies to assist followers in internalizing values. • Induce changes in values, attitudes and behavior using personal examples and expertise. • Exhibit leading behavior and will act to bring about change in others congruent with long-term objectives.	reporting structures. • Use command and control leadership through the application of formal administrative policies and procedures. • Maintain strict segregation of management and the working class. • Ensure jobs are defined strictly by the job descriptions (functional specialization) and not by the individuals who perform them. • Resist change preferring the status quo. • Avoid making decisions especially when there are no corporate policy guidelines. • Ensure that decisions are made slowly and carefully to maintain stability and order despite the speed of change in the external environment.

Conclusion

We are not seeking to claim that Renaissance Leadership describes every aspect of leadership required at all levels of a modern, performance focused organization. But we are suggesting that the framework we provide in this book is one that is robust, insightful and sufficiently focused to permit an organization wanting to achieve high performance to do so. These comparisons with other leadership frameworks show that we have learned from different attempts to capture modern leadership and that we are extending leadership thinking with new constructs which build from the solid work of others.

Chapter 11: A Comprehensive Expedition – The Next Stages of the Journey

"Mountains seem to have been built for the human race
Serving both as their schools and their cathedrals
Full of treasures of illuminated manuscripts for the scholar
Kindly in simple lessons for the worker
Quiet in pale cloisters for the thinker
Glorious in holiness for the worshipper
Mountains are great cathedrals of the earth
With their gates of rock and their pavements of cloud
Choirs of stream and stone, altars of snow and vaults of purple,
transversed by the continual stars"

—*John Ruskin*

In the early 1990's, work on the development of renaissance leadership began at the Banff Centre in the Rocky Mountains of Alberta, Canada and has continued, with many detours and base camps, ever since. We refer to this work as "an expedition", since the metaphor is apt. It describes a journey seeking to chart emerging territories of knowledge, behaviours, values and perceptions shaping our world.

In this expedition we have been helped by many who have helped outfit the journey with needed concepts, tools and maps, which have enabled the journey to continue. We have also faced roadblocks and had to climb mountains to overcome challenges. In this final chapter we want to chart some aspects of this journey while, at the same time, demonstrating the veracity of the renaissance leadership framework as an overarching "guide-light" for this expedition. We will summarize both some milestones in our expedition to date and describe the new expedition we are now actively preparing.

Milestones to Date

The expedition has had a number of key milestones on its journey of discovery. Key amongst these were:

- The Alberta government challenged the Innovation Expedition team to design and implement a public dialogue (called the Alberta Roundtables) on the theme: *"What will it take to make Alberta an Innovation-Driven Society?* This innovative initiative, which drew on individuals and ideas from all sectors and disciplines, engaged over 1,000 community leaders directly and over 20,000 individuals indirectly. It created the map for most of the efforts by the Alberta government over the next decade to develop a culture of innovation in Alberta.

- The Roundtables in Alberta served as a laboratory for testing the initial performance improvement ideas of the Innovation Expedition Inc. and stimulated the team's flagship program—the Challenge Dialogue System (CDS)™ which, since then, has developed a powerful capacity for helping diverse stakeholders to collaborate and innovate in accomplishing complex tasks. The CDS System™ has now been used by a great many organizations to explore key issues, challenges and opportunities.

- The learning from the Alberta Roundtables and the cross-cultural leadership work of the Banff Centre became the core of the Innovation Expedition's efforts to help individuals, organizations and political jurisdictions develop cultures which drive improved performance by unleashing innovation. CDS™ has been used by clients in various sectors throughout North America, as well as in Europe, Africa, Japan, Southeast Asia, and China. In addition, insightful interventions and supporting activities in many of the Fortune 500 companies of the world – Textron, EMC^2, Oracle,

Barclays Bank, Heinz, Debenhams (UK), Tesco, Citibank, Boots (UK) – to name just a few, provided some of the "raw" materials which helped us define the nature of renaissance leadership.

- In 2000, a group of business consultants from an eight-country network, working from an organizational base in Sweden (the Foresight Group), were stimulated by Don Simpson to examine the new realities of what he suggested was a modern-day Renaissance dealing with the transition from an industrial to a knowledge age. This group engaged in an online "journey of the mind" to consider the nature and location of today's Renaissance Cities which are serving as catalytic supports for the Renaissance Leaders and the innovative organizations they are creating. This Dialogue culminated in a workshop in Stockholm, in which participants explored whether it could be considered a Renaissance City.

- The Renaissance concept over the next few years provided a stimulating context for the ongoing work of the Innovation Expedition. It was discussed with thought leaders in various part of the world who were also beginning to explore the idea from their own organizational perspectives. For example, our colleagues at the European Foundation for Management Development (EFMD) in Brussels, over a decade ago, drew on the Renaissance concepts outlined here for the design of a major event.

- In 2007, Gay Haskins, the Dean of Executive Education at the Saïd Business School, invited Don Simpson to explore how to organize and input some creative elements from the work of the Innovation Expedition into the school's global Advanced Management Programme (AMP). He was assisted in this work by Jan Simpson, Stephen Murgatroyd and Doug James who each worked as "outfitters" for this leg of the expedition, ensuring that appropriate resources were available.

- In 2009 and again in 2010, Stephen Murgatroyd has worked with senior executives participating in Athabasca University's online Executive MBA program and has explored with them the links between knowledge, innovation, learning and performance in a renaissance age. They have used the ideas of Renaissance Leadership as a lens through which to review the issues of how high performing organizations need new leadership to be globally competitive.

- Since November 2007, the Innovation Expedition Inc. team has been building on the key learning from these two interventions at the AMP to start developing a flexible, global Renaissance Leadership initiative. Significant steps have been made in 2009 and 2010 to engage a number of clients, as well as other leadership programmes (the Schulich Business School at York University in Toronto, and WHU in Koblenz) in further explorations for launching a broad-based Renaissance Leadership Programme and for stimulating the development of a global community of practice around the concept of Renaissance Leadership for the Knowledge Age

- From 2007 through to 2010, Stephen Murgatroyd has been working with a variety of organizations, including school boards, teacher unions and others, to develop an understanding of the implications of renaissance leadership for the work of schools, especially schools in Canada. He has been supported in this work by the Alberta Teachers Association.

- Stephen Murgatroyd, working with others in the Innovation Expedition Inc., has also been instrumental in helping to reshape the innovation system in Alberta and

Ontario, using insights gained from the substantive work of the Alberta Round Tables as well as other consultative work.

- The launch of a program in 2010, focused on renaissance leadership in Canada, has been built around a group of Founding Members—organizations from different sectors and from nonprofits, research centres and government agencies, that share a commitment to *Rethink the Future* and to create a culture of collaboration and innovation in their organizations.

We summarize these key activities – there are many more – so as to demonstrate that our thinking as described here is anchored in practice and experience. Subsequent materials will provide practical resources and insights into making renaissance leadership work in a variety of settings.

Creating the Core Elements of a Renaissance Leadership Program

The Renaissance Expedition is both a model and a metaphor. As a model, the Renaissance Expedition is a cost-effective, collaborative model for co-creating, testing, sharing and promoting a leadership model that speaks to the need for:

- Systems Thinking (Integration and Convergence)
- Global Cross-Cultural Perspectives
- Respect for Diversity
- Tolerance for Ambiguity and Skills in Managing Ambiguity
- Ability to collaborate and create networks for action
- Shifting from Command and Control to Encourage and Empower

- Driving organizational high performance with an attention to a Triple Bottom Line approach – aimed at ensuring initiatives led to improved economic, social and environmental outcomes.

As a metaphor, it is positioning the knowledge economy as a new world (culture) and positioning the Expeditions as cross-cultural experiences to help leaders prepare themselves and others for success in this world.

We are now developing a focused, comprehensive and customized approach to leadership development, which we call the Comprehensive Expedition.

The Comprehensive Expedition

This Comprehensive Expedition is intended to serve initially as a conceptual organizing vehicle for an evolving Renaissance Leadership Program. It is designed for leaders interested in a sustained (six months to one year), part-time personal and professional development initiative which presents a synergistic alternative or a supportive addition to traditional academy-based programs. Our comprehensive expedition also challenges participants to play an active role as an Explorer in shaping and helping to co-create a learning and leadership experience that is customized to their particular leadership needs. The various elements, challenges and learning experiences offered in this Comprehensive Expedition are available to be used individually in any short term (modular) initiatives organized by Founding Sponsors or by clients of the Renaissance Leadership Program – the name we have given to the Comprehensive Expedition.

The program involves: (a) base camps where participants deepen understanding and master skills; (b) scouting parties, where participants immerse themselves in other organizations so as to better understand their own; (c) inspired conversations, where we provide access to members of a global network of renaissance leaders who will share their experience, knowledge and understanding in a way that challenges participants to move beyond their normative responses to the challenges they face; and (d) summit sessions in which participants will share and evaluate their learning. There will also be extensive access to e-learning and online resources. We show this framework in the figure below.

This program draws on the power of the expedition metaphor, described earlier, by viewing this knowledge economy as if it were an intriguing new place for us to explore and understand. The Comprehensive Expedition is thus organized as a cross-cultural learning experience based on key learning from history to help oneself and others prepare for success in this new renaissance world.

Our initial focus will be on three aspects of this new world – corporate social responsibility, strategic foresight and innovation. The idea is that participants will be actively engaged in the co-creation of the knowledge and skills they require to better understand these three domains of their work while at the same time using their developing knowledge and skills to solve real and substantive challenges which the organization they work for has identified as mission critical. Rather than looking at case studies, participants will work collaboratively to leverage opportunities within their organization for change. This is building on similar work we completed with Textron, Oracle and the Metropolitan Housing Trust (UK). It also leverages the expertise within the Expedition of using technology in support of real learning.

A Focus on Improving Individual and Organizational Performance by Unleashing Innovation

The Renaissance Leadership Program is intended to provide participants with an exciting opportunity for customized, accelerated, personal learning and an opportunity to dramatically expand their network of connections with other outstanding leaders globally who are Rethinking the Future™ and searching for creative responses to the complex challenges of a fast-changing, highly competitive knowledge based economy.

It will help them to strengthen an integrated package of **Knowing, Doing** and **Being** skills required to spark dramatic improvements in individual and organizational performance by unleashing innovation. This journey is intended to support efforts of leaders to function as major motivators and catalysts for helping their organizations transform themselves to survive and thrive in a global knowledge-based economy.

The Four Performance Challenges to Address During the Renaissance Leadership Program

As part of the expedition, participants are required to identify four performance challenges. With the help and assistance of the Expedition Crew (their guides, coaches and mentors), their personal mentor, inputs from their fellow Explorers and from our global network of colleagues – a group we call the global mentoring team, they will work as a team to achieve specific outcomes. They are expected to draw on the insights from the journey to support their efforts to address their personal performance challenges in the following four categories:

- *An organizational performance challenge*—select a complex challenge in the organization which will be addressed during the Expedition. In most cases, this will be provided to the participants by the senior management, after some negotiation.

- *A mentoring challenge*—by selecting a younger leader in the organization with whom participants plan to share their learning from the Expedition in the role of a mentor (and at the same time strengthening their own skills of mentoring).

- *A strategic communications challenge*—selecting a successful innovator in the global mentoring team to interview with the intention of capturing and articulating their story, highlighting the lessons to be learned and then being skilled in sharing these lessons with colleagues in the organization and beyond in a way that inspires them.

- *A social innovation challenge*—having selected an organization that addresses a major social challenge that interests participants, get engaged directly with this group in a manner that produces mutual benefits. The social challenges may be local, national or global and the direct involvement of a participant or group of participants may involve a few hours, a few days or several weeks. From experience, working in a different kind of organization challenged assumptions and enabled participants to fully explore their own "taken for granted" assumptions about how organizations function and what leadership looks like.

What are the Operating Assumptions of this Program?

The assumptions we make about the process of learning should be clear. We assume adult learning to require a high degree of engagement, co-creation, exploration, real challenges that have authentic audiences and to be problem focused. While not averse to didactic teaching when appropriate, our focus is on learning through reflective action – what we refer to as "real learning". While skills can be taught, it is essential that they are also understood – hence the focus is always on context, mastery through challenge and team based work.

Here are our other key assumptions about this program:

- The type of leadership that drove organizational success in the industrial era will not be sufficient for the knowledge era.

- Leaders require an expanded portfolio of thinking, doing and being (relationship) skills to successfully grow high performing knowledge-based organizations.

- The concept of a Renaissance Leader is an apt metaphor because this shift to a knowledge economy is a significant period of rebirth akin to the great Renaissance periods of the past and shares with them an intense focus on learning and inquiry encompassing all aspects of human life.

- Our assumption is that to address the complex challenges of a global knowledge economy one requires an ability to build collaborative teams with the capacity to unleash innovation.

- Innovation can be taught through real learning.

- Innovation can be stimulated by engaging interactions among leaders from diverse sectors and providing them with an appropriate environment and stimulus for sharing challenges and stories of team experiences. Ideas and innovative solutions flow from these high level conversations which are seeded with high level questions. The conversations also lead to relationships and shared understanding.

- Once a clear challenge has been identified, work teams can be established to explore design ideas and action plans for driving improved performance. They may need to be shown and able to practice new-to-them skills.

- The Innovation Expedition brings to these interactions and the implementation efforts that follow:

  - a global perspective

  - a network of influential innovators

  - an objective view

  - distinctive mentoring skills

  - an extensive knowledge bank of principles, processes and tools for addressing complex tasks.

The various Expeditions organized within the Renaissance Leadership Program are positioned as cross-cultural learning experiences for understanding the knowledge economy and then learning how to prepare oneself and others for success in this world.

The Renaissance Leadership Program serves as a rallying point for efforts to organize and implement major change initiatives in organizations and in large systems.

The intent is to identify and support these leaders who are moved to action by awareness of the lessons from earlier Renaissance periods and by a desire to emulate the behaviour of some of these leadership heroes from an earlier age as well as their modern-day counterparts.

The program will be attractive to organizations that are seeking to transform themselves in order to survive and thrive in these turbulent times. The expeditions and related events organized by this Renaissance Leadership Program will be attractive to leaders who combine:

- an active curiosity about the world in all its complexity

- an eagerness to explore innovative approaches for dealing with the complex challenges they are facing in sustaining and growing their organization

- an openness for learning how to choose and successfully utilize new information and communication technologies to support performance improvement initiatives.

The comprehensive expedition is intended to assist these kinds of leaders in diverse types of organizations (business firms, research centres, government agencies, nonprofit social agencies, cultural groups and educational institutions). It is aimed at individuals who are committed to function as entrepreneurial, collaborative leaders with a capacity for driving dramatic improvements in organizational performance by unleashing innovation.

The program is equally relevant to executives from the private, public and not-for-profit sectors—and indeed starts from the premise that interaction among people with diverse perspectives and experience is a catalyst for breakthrough thinking and practical innovation.

What are the Potential Benefits Offered to Participants?

Participating organizations have access to:

- A powerful communications vehicle that can serve as a rallying call to unleash innovations aimed at creating organizations with the capacity to survive and thrive in uncertain times.

- A diverse but focused network of Founding Members, each of which is committed to:

  - rethinking the future™

  - building leadership capacity to create a culture of collaboration and innovation to implement that future

  - collaborating with other Founding Members of the Renaissance Network in order to quickly and effectively implement these transformations in a cost-effective manner

- A Global Mentoring Team of experienced and influential innovators who are committed to supporting the intentions, values and operating principles of the Renaissance Program.

- A comprehensive set of resources (processes, learning experiences, tools and other specialized support materials) that can be used to stimulate team actions addressing key performance challenges and to provide mentoring support for any actions that are undertaken.

- A virtual Renaissance Laboratory to support processes for undertaking quick, inexpensive global intelligence on potential innovations as well as providing support for designing projects and systems to support major transformations to drive improved performance.

Conclusion

Our next book will be a field guide to making renaissance leadership happen – providing insights, resources and support for the practice of renaissance leadership. It will be derived from our work with the Founding Members of the Renaissance Network and with those engaged in our Comprehensive Expedition. We are at work on this book now.

But here we have laid out the terrain of renaissance leadership and provided a context for the ongoing expedition.